Military Professionalism and the Early American Officer Corps
1789-1796

Christopher W. Wingate, Major, US Army
Fort Leavenworth, Kansas
2013

Combat Studies Institute Press
US Army Combined Arms Center
Fort Leavenworth, Kansas

Abstract

In September 2012, the Department of the Army published new capstone doctrine, Army Doctrine Publication 1 (ADP 1), *The Army,* in which the concept of military professionalism occupies an especially prominent place. Coinciding with the release of *The Army,* the Chief of Staff declared that 2013 features a focus on professionalism; entitled "America's Army – Our Profession," in an effort to better understand the idea of military professionalism.

Military history can and should contribute to an understanding of American military professionalism. Investigating the nature of professionalism in the officer corps serving during President George Washington's administration, the central argument of this study is that early Army leaders demonstrated a particularly American style of military professionalism. The early officer corps grappled with the same elements described by the Army's current doctrine as fundamentally characteristic of military professionalism: trust, expertise, service, esprit and stewardship. Understanding the strengths, weaknesses, challenges, and limitations of the early officer corps' approach to professionalism in light of these five key characteristics provides important background and a useful conceptual framework to more fully understand the American military tradition and today's doctrine concerning military professionalism.

Acknowledgments

Undertaking a project of this magnitude during a full-time school year required the assistance and patience of multiple people. I especially appreciate the professional and kind help of my chair, Dr. Richard Barbuto, as well as the two readers, Dr. Joseph Fischer and Dr. Ethan Rafuse. In addition, I thank the Art of War Scholars Program instructors, Dr. Sean Kalic, Dr. Scott Stephenson, and Dr. Fischer, for their encouragement and assistance in setting up research trips in support of my paper. Special thanks are due to the library staff at the Combined Arms Research Library at Fort Leavenworth and to my father, Mr. Henry Wingate, for their tremendous help in tracking down and obtaining often obscure primary sources. Last, but not least, I am thankful to my wife Bethany and my children, Robert and Clara, for their patience when I disappeared into my office many an evening to work on this project.

Table of Contents

Chapter 1
Introduction

As the United States Army emerges from over a decade of war, there is a renewed interest among Army leaders concerning the state of military professionalism and Officership. Thus, the Chief of Staff of the Army declared that the year 2013 features an emphasis on military professionalism, entitled "America's Army – Our Profession" with the goal of promoting understanding of professionalism and encouraging dedication to its obligations. This year-long campaign emphasizes the prominent inclusion of a description of military professionalism in the service's 2012 capstone doctrinal document, Army Doctrine Publication 1 (ADP 1), *The Army*. In this manual and in supporting Department of the Army publications, professionalism is defined as "a vocation comprised of experts certified in the ethical design, generation, support, and application of land combat power, serving under Civilian authority, entrusted to defend the Constitution and the rights and interests of the American people." *The Army* describes five essential characteristics of military professionalism: trust, military expertise, honorable service, esprit, and stewardship. In addition to these characteristics, authentic professionalism calls for competence, commitment and character.[1]

Military history can and should provide context for this renewed focus on professionalism. Historians and military practitioners have provided such context for over a century, yet surprisingly few have concentrated their efforts on the very first years of the United States Army, when the United States military establishment first formed and when the tradition and ethos of the nation's Army were initially established. Instead, since the posthumous publication in 1904 of Brigadier General Emory Upton's seminal work *The Military Policy of the United States*, many historians and theorists have accepted his argument that prior to the late 1800s; the American Army Officer Corps was largely composed of amateurs. Other prominent scholars look to the years following the War of 1812 for indications of professional development. Few have looked earlier to investigate the development of professional characteristics; most scholars appear to regard pre-1812 Officers as amateurs.[2] This dismissal of the early American Army Officer Corps as unprofessional is unfortunate for two key reasons. First, such a dismissal is historically inaccurate. Second, this characterization of the early Officer Corps as unprofessional poses a danger to a thorough understanding of American military professionalism because it arbitrarily separates current perceptions of professionalism from the traditions of professionalism developed by the nation's original Officer Corps.

This study's central argument is that during President George Washington's administration, the Army Officer Corps developed a limited but very real and particularly American style of military professionalism. Contrary to the belief of most historians who disregard the notion of professionalism developing before the War of 1812, the early Officer Corps quickly developed significant professional characteristics. Such professionalism developed alongside the amateurism that was also evident during the officer corps' first decades. Central to this argument is an acceptance of the broad definition of professionalism laid out in *The Army*. This broad description of military professionalism is valuable and important for it avoids much of the peripheral and semantic baggage raised by an anachronistic comparison between the modern use of the word professional and its earlier usage. The Army's broad definition allows a focus on the core of the meaning of military professionalism, disallowing a hasty rejection of any professionalism within the early Officer Corps simply because, for instance, officers did not matriculate at a military academy. Instead, this definition encourages examining professionalism in light of the fundamental and enduring characteristics of trust, expertise, service, esprit, and stewardship.

This thesis examines the nature of the professionalism of the Army's officer corps from its establishment in 1789 with the ratification of the US Constitution, until 1796 as Washington's presidency and the Northwest Indian War ended. This seven-year period was an extraordinary time for the nation's young Army and its leadership as it confronted multiple simultaneous challenges to the development of officer professionalism. These included: deep-seated philosophical tensions between the new nation's need for security and a suspicion of standing armies; a critical lack of government funds; a responsibility to provide security and assist in the governance of a vast frontier with extremely limited resources; the requirement to formulate appropriate civil-military relations; and a need to combine the military efforts of volunteer, militia and regular forces organizationally and operationally. The Officer Corps developed in the midst of simultaneously dealing with these challenges and confronting the new nation's first military opponent – the Confederated Tribes of the Northwest Territory.

In order to examine the professionalism of the early American Officer Corps, this study employs a systematic methodology. After a brief historical overview of the Army's history between 1789 and 1796 in the introduction, it examines the early American Officer Corps in relation to each characteristic of professionalism – trust, expertise, service, esprit, and stewardship. Because of the immense influence of Washington and the first Secretary of War, Henry Knox, each chapter investigates the nature of the pertinent characteristic from the senior leader level down to the junior officer level. The existence of a significant body of primary sources, backed by the use of secondary literature, allows for a direct examination of the nature of professionalism within the early American Officer Corps. The collections of the papers of both Washington and Knox are extensive, as are compendiums of the correspondence and orderly books of the three primary general officers during this era: Brevet Brigadier General Josiah Harmar, Major General Arthur St. Clair, and Major General Anthony Wayne.[3] In addition, the court of inquiry and congressional inquiry held after the defeats suffered by Harmar and St. Clair provide valuable evidence as do various reports found in the *American State Papers* collection.[4] Extant orderly books from Fort Knox and from General Wayne's command, as well as extensive correspondence between senior and military leaders, provide important help in understanding the daily challenges faced by the Officer Corps during this early period.[5] A substantial number of primary sources from field and junior officers provided critical insight into the Officer Corps. In total, this study examined 12 journals from officers serving during this period and several collections of letters and other correspondence. In addition to these primary sources, secondary sources, including both general histories of the period and biographies of critical figures, provide an essential background.[6] As in any historical inquiry, the type and source of available evidence limit and frame this work. In choosing representative figures and examples within the Officer Corps, this study attempts to retain a breadth of understanding of the entire Officer Corps so as not to generalize the state of the entire body by a few elite figures.

Thus, this methodology seeks both breadth and depth in painting a collective portrait of the nature of the military professionalism of the early American Officer Corps by the combined use of primary and secondary sources. Before beginning a chapter-by-chapter examination of the five characteristics of military professionalism, a brief historical overview of the Army between 1789 and 1796 may be useful.

With the adoption of the Constitution in 1789, the new nation inherited from the Confederation a tiny regular force of 700 soldiers, spread throughout the American frontier, from Georgia to the Canadian border. Tasked with staffing the frontier forts that the British would be vacating in accordance with the 1783 Treaty of Paris, this small force also attempted to keep an uneasy peace between settlers and Indians, deter foreign infringement on national territory, and maintain a semblance of order in the absence of an adequate civil government. Led by Pennsylvanian Brevet Brigadier General Josiah Harmar, the force included 44 officers.[7]

Legally incorporated by Congress in August of 1789, the Army of 700 regulars faced increasing levels of resistance from Indians of the Northwest Territory, consisting primarily of lands north and northwest of the Ohio River and consisting of present-day Ohio, Indiana, Illinois, and parts of Michigan.[8] Prior to 1783, Britain claimed the area using allied tribes to limit American settlement. The Treaty of Paris of 1783, in ending the American Revolution, ceded these lands to the United States without considering tribal rights and claims to these same lands. Hungry for land and the financial benefits of it to the new nation, and mindful that the great majority of the Indian tribes had allied themselves with Britain in the Revolution, United States leaders largely considered these tribes as conquered nations and their lands as legitimately won in war and validated by the Treaty of Paris. With this attitude, conflict was perhaps inevitable as the lure of land increasingly drew American settlers westward. The post-war continuing presence of British forces in the area, reluctant to let go of the area's lucrative fur trade, was legitimized by American delinquency in fulfilling treaty requirements pertaining to loyalist property and remuneration. In order to maintain this trade, British leaders in Canada ordered positions maintained in the Northwest Territory and encouraged and equipped Indian resistance to American settlers. Already having lost the rich hunting grounds of Kentucky to American settlers by 1789, Indian tribes needed little encouragement to strike at the increasing numbers of settlers north of the Ohio River.

The Washington administration also wanted to avoid settlement north of the Ohio River but for different reasons.[9] These lands, claimed by the new American Government and by several States, were potentially a rich source of badly needed revenue, if sold to settlers or land companies, as well as a way to pay off debts owed to Revolutionary War veterans. Settlers moving in before the land could be surveyed and advertised and sold, threatened the land use envisioned by the Washington administration. Furthermore, such encroachment raised the risk of general conflict with the strong Miami and Shawnee tribes, a conflict which would likely require an expensive build-up of military forces in the region. Thus in 1789, one of General Harmar's missions was to keep American settlers from crossing north of the Ohio River to settle. With such a tiny force, this was doomed to failure and Indian raids repeatedly struck increasing numbers of settlements. These settlements and raids led to a vicious cycle of escalation, particularly due to the brutal methods used by both Indian raiding parties and volunteer and militia retaliatory expeditions. Harmar watched helplessly as the conflict escalated. The administration's sincere attempts at peaceful conciliation with the tribes failed by late 1789 due to a striking variance in Indian and settler perceptions of land ownership. By late 1789, settlement cries for protection from Indian raids and a realization that peace talks were failing, spurred the United States Army's first campaign.

In late 1789, Northwest Territory Governor Arthur St. Clair requested federal help to resolve the "constant hostilities between the Indians who live upon the river Wabash and the people of Kentucky."[10] In response, Washington and Knox pushed through Congress a slight increase in the size of the regular Army, to 1,200 soldiers including 57 officers, organized in one United States Regiment of Infantry and an artillery battalion for a three-year period. In addition, Washington gave the governor permission to call forth necessary militia forces for the coming campaign.[11] In early 1790, Washington granted permission to St. Clair to mobilize these troops. Additionally, he ordered 1,500 militia from Kentucky and Pennsylvania to join regular forces consolidating at Fort Washington and Fort Knox. Giving wide latitude to Governor St. Clair and General Harmar to plan the campaign, Knox directed them to conduct rapid operations in order to "exhibit to the Wabash Indians our power to punish them for their positive depredations, for their conniving at the depredations of others, and for their refusing to treat with the United States when invited thereto."[12]

Conceiving a two-column strike into the region bounded by the Wabash, Miamim, and St. Mary's Rivers, St. Clair and Harmar initiated operations in September 1790.[13] A diversionary threat northward along the Wabash River by Major Hamtramck's force of approximately 350 soldiers (approximately half of whom were militia) would draw attention from the main effort by Harmar northward to the central Miami villages 150 miles north of Fort Washington. Some 1,300 militiamen under Kentucky Militia Colonel John Hardin joined the 350 regular troops under Harmar for this attack against hostile Indian villages. As the main body marched north, Indians under Miami Chief Little Turtle ambushed and badly defeated a raiding party with the loss of over 100 soldiers. Angered by this loss, Harmar responded by organizing an attack on the main enemy village of Kekionga. However, a second ambush by Little Turtle surprised the attackers while burning the village, and surrounded by approximately 1,000 Indian warriors, the American force suffered another defeat, resulting in several hundred casualties. Faced with this defeat and low on food and supplies, Harmar ordered a retreat back to Fort Washington near the town of Cincinnati in late October 1790. Meanwhile, Hamtramck's force had not encountered any hostile Indians, and beset by supply shortages returned to Fort Knox without engaging the enemy. While Harmar claimed to have accomplished part of his mission by burning a great quantity of enemy crops and villages, it was clear to both St. Clair and the Washington administration that the campaign had failed and only emboldened the hostile tribes.

In early 1791, Washington and Knox pushed for another increase in the size of the regular Army to about 2,000 soldiers and 78 officers, organized into a first and second regiment of United States Infantry, supported by a battalion of artillery. The government intended to supplement this enlarged force with 1,500 militiamen from Kentucky for the next campaign. Unsatisfied by Harmar's performance, Washington turned to veterans of the Revolutionary War, naming Arthur St. Clair the Army's new commanding general and General Richard Butler as second-in-command in March of 1791. Weak recruiting and supply efforts hampered preparations for this second campaign. Under pressure from the administration to act before some of the short-term soldiers' enlistments expired, St. Clair ordered an advance in late 1791.

This combined force, consisting of approximately 2,300 men, including about 700 militiamen under militia Colonel William Oldham, experienced tremendous logistical difficulties which caused great dissension within the force and led to high levels of desertion, demands to be let go as enlistment terms expired, and finally the defection of over half the militia halfway through the march north. St. Clair responded to this mutiny by ordering his Second US Regiment under Hamtramck to intercept the errant militia while continuing his march north with only approximately 1,400 soldiers. By early November, this diminished force led by an ill St. Clair pushed toward the site of Harmar's defeat, burning villages and crops on the march. Led by chiefs Little Turtle and Blue Jacket, the estimated 1,200 warriors from various tribes of the region, supported by British military advisors, retired from the advancing American Army until reaching the northern reaches of the Wabash River. At dawn the next day, Indian warriors again badly surprised the American Army. Quickly demoralized and losing most sense of discipline, St. Clair's surrounded force suffered appalling casualties, only escaping total annihilation by a sudden attack through the Indian lines and sudden retreat. One of the most decisive defeats in the history of the United States Army, St. Clair's campaign resulted in the loss of 630 killed and hundreds more wounded and nearly all Army supplies lost. Casualties included 69 of the 124 officers present, including General Richard Butler. The impact of this loss was of course, the exact opposite of the intent, with the victorious tribes emboldened and growing in power and influence.

In shock over the disaster, the Washington administration turned to a three-pronged strategy to counter the invigorated Indian enemy.[14] First, intensified diplomatic efforts sought a negotiated peace with the hostile tribes. Second, through diplomacy, the government attempted to cut off British support for enemy tribes. Third, leaders reorganized and enlarged the Army. This last exertion involved the administration pushing through another slight increase in the size of the Army to approximately 2,500 troops, now organized in a combined arms framework and called the Legion of the United States. After pushing St. Clair to resign his command, Washington and Knox turned to another Revolutionary War comrade, Major General Anthony Wayne, to command the newly built Legion. Assisting him would be his second in command, Major General Charles Scott, leading the Kentucky Militia and Brigadier General James Wilkinson, leading one of the regiments of the new American Army.

Intensive peace efforts in the latter parts of 1792 and throughout 1793 provided Wayne time to build and train an effective force. When peace efforts finally failed in late 1793, Wayne initiated the third major campaign of the Northwest Indian War. Embarking on a northern march over the same ground of the two previous campaigns, Wayne led his combined Army of 2,500 regulars and 1,500 mounted Kentucky militia toward the hostile Indian villages, in order to destroy villages and crops and draw the Indians into a decisive battle. Despite supply shortages and sickness, Wayne's Army continued past Kekionga and Grand Glaize in good shape, burning crops and villages along the way. Continuing northward toward Lake Erie and the British-held stronghold at Fort Miami, Wayne's scouts identified the main Indian force of approximately 1,500 warriors, led by the Shawnee Chief Blue Jacket, and assisted by scores of Canadian militia and advised by British military agents. On the morning of 20 August 1794, Wayne ordered his combined force to attack the Indian warriors who were prepared in fallen trees along the Maumee River. The mixed attack of the regular infantry supported by artillery and the mounted militia soon broke the Indian forces which fled toward Fort Miami. The British regular forces manning Fort Miami refused admittance to the fleeing Indian warriors, ensuring a decisive victory for General Wayne's Army.

In the aftermath of the Battle of Fallen Timbers, the chastened Indian tribes, now understandably distrustful of their former British allies, accepted the peace proposals offered by Wayne and signed the Treaty of Greeneville in 1795. This treaty forced the Indians to accept American ownership of most of the lands of the Northwest Territory, consolidating Indian tribal lands to the area just south of the Great Lakes. One of the most decisive American Army victories, Wayne's campaign opened the majority of the Northwest Territory to American settlement and led to peace with regional Indian tribes for over the next decade. Encouraged by this triumph, the administration and Congress agreed to continue the force structure and size of the Legion for an additional three years. For the first time, the United States Army gained acceptance as an expanded and regular peacetime force essential to national defense.

One final introductory word may be useful. The intent of this thesis is not to investigate a possible direct link in the development from these early periods to the present day. Given the instability that characterized the Army in the initial decades, such a project is doubtful and is certainly beyond the scope of this thesis. Rather, this study proposes to examine the nature of military professionalism of the early American officer corps, focusing on the challenges and responses related to trust, expertise, service, esprit, and stewardship. In this way, this study may provide some insight into the overall conceptual framework and intentions, thoughts, desires, understandings, actions, tensions, problems, and solutions facing the leaders of the new American Army as they consciously and unconsciously formed the first United States military tradition. Such an understanding may inform today's Officer Corps, the Army, and American society, providing all a better understanding of a shared heritage. This may prove useful in the pursuit of a deeper understanding of American military professionalism.

Notes

1.   Military professionalism is described in Headquarters, Department of the Army, Army Doctrine Publication 1, *The Army* (Washington, DC: Government Printing Office, September, 2012), http://armypubs.army.mil/doctrine/ADP_1.html (accessed 12 May 2013), ch 2. A supporting document is Headquarters, Army Training and Doctrine Command, *The Army Profession: 2012, After More than a Decade of Conflict,* Center for the Army Profession and Ethic, October 2011, http://cape.army.mil/repository/ProArms/Army%20Profession%20Pamphlet.pdf (accessed 12 May 2013). The purpose of the 2013 focus on Army professionalism is described in Headquarters, Army Training and Doctrine Command, *America's Army – Our Profession Information Paper,* Center for the Army Profession and Ethic, October 2012, http://cape.army.mil/AAOP/AAOP%20 Overview/repository/info%20paper/20121004_AA-OP_Information_Paper_ (Final_Approved_v2).pdf (accessed 12 May 2013).

2.   See chapter two of this thesis for a historiographical review of the concept of military professionalism in the American military, starting with Upton's influential work.

3.   Washington's papers can be found almost in their entirety at George Washington, *The George Washington Papers,* Alderman Library, University of Virginia, Charlottesville, VA, http://gwpapers.virginia.edu (accessed 7 May 2013). Harmar's correspondence as the commanding general from 1789 to 1790 is reprinted in Gayle Thornbrough, ed., *Outpost on the Wabash, 1787-1791; Letters of Brigadier General Josiah Harmar and Major John Francis Hamtramck. and Other Letters and Documents* (Indianapolis, IN: Indiana Historical Society, 1957. St. Clair's papers are reprinted in William H. Smith, ed., *The St. Clair Papers: The Life and Public Services of Arthur St. Clair : Soldier of the Revolutionary War, President of the Continental Congress ; and Governor of the North-Western Territory with His Correspondence and Other Papers,* 2 vols. (Cincinnati, OH: R. Clarke, 1882). Wayne's papers for the pertinent period are reprinted in Richard C. Knopf, ed., *Anthony Wayne, a Name in Arms: Soldier, Diplomat, Defender of Expansion Westward of a Nation; the Wayne-Knox-Pickering-McHenry Correspondence* (Westport, CT: Greenwood Press, 1975).

4.   Records of Harmar's court of inquiry and St. Clair's congressional investigation are reprinted in United States, *American State Papers, Military Affairs, Volume I* (New York, NY: Arno, 1979).

5.   Milo M. Quaife, "Fort Knox Orderly Book, 1793-97," *Indiana Magazine of History* 32, no. 2 (1936): 137-169 and Richard C. Knopf, ed. *Orderly Books for the United States Legion Vols. I-IV Incl.* (Columbus, OH: Anthony Wayne Parkway Board, Ohio State Museum, 1955).

6.   The bibliography lists the journals, histories, and biographies employed by this study.

7.   Numbers and ranks of officers in this study generally derive from documents in United States, *American State Papers: Military Affairs* and the comprehensive and invaluable, Francis Heitman, *Historical Register and Dictionary of the United States Army: from its Organization, September 29, 1789, to March 2, 1903* (Washington, DC: Government Printing Office, 1903).

8.   Especially helpful in the general history of the Northwest Territory and Indian-American affairs is R. Douglas Hurt, *The Ohio Frontier: Crucible of the Old Northwest, 1720-1830* (Bloomington, IN: Indiana University Press, 1998).

9.   The Washington administration's struggles with the Indian tribes in the Northwest Territory are well described in Wiley Sword, *President Washington's Indian War: The Struggle for the Old Northwest, 1790-1795* (Norman, OK: Oklahoma University Press, 1985).

10.   United States, *American State Papers, Indian Affairs, Volume I* (New York, NY: Arno, 1979), St. Clair to Washington, 58.

11.   In addition to primary sources and Sword's general history of the war, Harry Ward, *The Department of War, 1781-1795* (Pittsburgh, PA: University of Pittsburgh Press, 1962) is especially useful for information on the army's organization and structure throughout the war.

12.   William Smith, *The St. Clair Papers,* Knox to St. Clair, 19 September 1790, 182.

13.   In addition to primary sources and Sword's general history of the war, William H. Guthman, *March to Massacre: A History of the First Seven Years of the United States Army, 1784-1791* (New York, NY: McGraw Hill, 1975) is useful for its coverage of both Harmar's and St. Clair's campaigns.

14.   In addition to primary sources and the secondary sources already cited, Alan D. Gaff, *Bayonets in the Wilderness: Anthony Wayne's Legion in the Old Northwest* (Norman, OK: University of Oklahoma Press, 2004) is a valuable source for information on the final and decisive campaign of the Northwest Indian War.

Chapter 2
Historiography

Stuck unobtrusively between the Armies of the Revolutionary War and the War of 1812, the 1790s United States Army has attracted relatively little direct attention from military historians. The professionalism of this force has been largely ignored or dismissed. Still, a survey in a historiography sense of pertinent scholarship since the late 19th century illustrates the scholarly understanding of the first American Army and is therefore useful in framing this thesis.[1]

The first influential historical work with a bearing on professionalism and the early American Army came from the pen of General Emory Upton, a decorated Union veteran of the Civil War and post-war commandant of the United States Military Academy. In 1875, US Army Commanding General William Sherman dispatched Upton on a wide-ranging foreign trip in order to bring home recommendations on improving the United States Army. This trip resulted in the 1878 publication of *The Armies of Asia and Europe* and included strong recommendations for changes to the American Army in order to capitalize on Upton's observations abroad. Upton's experiences and studies also led him to work on his historical Magnus opus, *The Military Policy of the United States*. This work, unfinished at his death in 1881, was ordered published by Secretary of War Elihu Root in 1904, as part of his Army reform program. Upton's works clearly indicate a belief that the early American military establishment was characterized by a disastrous lack of military professionalism including officer incompetence, indiscipline, and confusion, and intermingling of civil and military responsibilities and spheres.

Upton scathingly wrote that an unreasonable fear of standing armies and military professionalism, and a corresponding reliance upon amateur militia and volunteer units in the Revolutionary and post-Revolutionary years, condemned the United States to long and expensive wars and "almost wrought the ruin of our cause."[2] Citing George Washington's statement in the aftermath of the 1776 Long Island debacle that placing "dependence upon militia is assuredly resting upon a broken staff," Upton claimed that "up to the Mexican War there was little that was glorious in our military history" due to a lack of American military professionalism.[3] Rejecting the idea that militia or volunteer officers were able to lead modern armies effectively, Upton urged that all of American military history through the Civil War showed the dangers of relying on any but regular and professional military leadership. In doing so, he advocated absorbing lessons especially from the Prussian model of officer professionalism with a corresponding clear division between civilian and military spheres of authority. This latter conclusion led directly to his recommendation for broader military authority in executing military operations.[4]

Upton's historical interpretation, championed by Root and successive Army leaders in the early 20th century, had a profound influence on future scholars. Discussions of professionalism have often been framed by acceptance or rejection of his theses regarding the nature of early American military professionalism. His interpretation was largely accepted in the early 20th century. For example, Charles and Mary Beard in their influential work *The Rise of American Civilization,* cite Upton while claiming the American Revolution illustrated the incompetence of unprofessional military forces.[5] Other early proponents of Upton's interpretation that the early American military establishment suffered from a lack of military professionalism included influential officer-scholars William Ganoe and Trevor Depuy.[6]

The first significant challenge to Upton's claims came from another officer-historian, General John McCauley Palmer. A World War I veteran, close advisor to General John Pershing in the aftermath of the war and later an advisor to General George Marshall during World War II, Palmer rejected Upton's conclusions that the citizen-soldier was unreliable. Palmer argued that with some amount of training and discipline, non-regular American military forces showed an ability to quickly become highly efficient. While accepting the need for some of Upton's recommendations, such as a better trained militia and the creation of a general staff, Palmer rejected Upton's conclusions that only full-time regular Army officers could be relied upon to effectively lead American armies. In the midst of World War II, Palmer argued that giving active-duty professional soldiers a monopoly on military leadership was a dramatic and dangerous departure from American military tradition and that such a monopoly would lead to the establishment of the large standing Army so feared by the founders of the United States. Such a monopoly, said Palmer, would repudiate the type of Army founded by Washington in the early republic, one that relied upon citizen-soldiers closely tied to American society. Palmer emphasized that "an enduring government by the people must include an Army of the people among its institutions."[7]

By World War II, Palmer and Marshall were convinced of the need to reiterate that the American military establishment was founded on the citizen-soldier concept and not the Prusso-German model championed by Upton's followers. With Marshall's backing, in 1943 Palmer published

America in Arms, urging a historical interpretation in which early American military history did not prove that militia forces were inevitably ineffective, but rather that an adequately trained body of citizen-soldiers had in the past, and could in the future, win the nation's wars.[8] Victory could thus be obtained, said Palmer, as it had in all former American wars – with a small force of regulars providing oversight for training and administration during peacetime and a large militia and volunteer force called out as needed for national defense. In this work, Palmer emphasized George Washington's proposals for the post-Revolutionary American military in his 1783 "Sentiments on a Peace Establishment" in which the retiring Revolutionary War commander in chief called for a small "regular and standing force" to supplement a large and well-organized militia, which Washington termed the "great bulwark of our Liberties and independence." [9]

In his rejection of what he termed the Sherman-Upton doctrine that only a larger and regular force was a reliable foundation for defense, Palmer warned that establishing a European-style professional military would entail a sharp departure from the practice of the early republic's military establishment. A large standing Army would tend to lead to a strict separation of professional regular officers from the larger society, which would violate the citizen-soldier concept articulated by Washington in his famous statement that "when we assumed the soldier, we did not lay aside the citizen."[10] Finally, a strictly professional military establishment threatened to compromise the nation's heritage of civilian control over the military.[11]

In the second half of the 20th century, academic historians began to more thoroughly investigate the nature of American military professionalism, which until this time had been dominated by officer-scholars like Upton and Palmer. Yet, as historian E. Wayne Carp persuasively notes, such was the influence of these two generals that throughout the 20th century, military historians continually responded to their arguments, often being placed into "Uptonian" or "Palmerian" camps.[12]

In 1957, Samuel Huntington established himself as a firm proponent of many aspects of Upton's thought with the publication of his hugely influential *The Soldier and the State: The Theory and Politics of Civil-Military Relations*.[13] Huntington, a political theorist, claimed that "prior to 1800 there was no such thing as a professional officer corps."[14] This was particularly true in America where, according to Huntington, the liberal political thought of the founders with their fear of a standing Army and separate professional body of military officers, ensured a reliance on amateur military leaders and establishments. Huntington believed that the United States military was only able to professionalize the officer corps in the aftermath of the Civil War, when leaders like Sherman and Upton took advantage of the relative isolation of the officer corps from society to inculcate a professional subculture distinct from the larger American society. He argued that only after 1865 did the American Army finally follow in the footsteps of the Prussian model. Prior to this, the American military establishment was distracted by an unprofessional focus on purely technical and populist concerns, like exploration or popular engineering projects. In addition, the citizen-soldier concept so dear to the founders led to high levels of political involvement by military leaders (and seemingly a correspondingly high level of military involvement by political leaders), which delayed the American establishment of military professionalism.[15]

Huntington advocated a rather narrow view of professionalism, viewing the profession of arms as being properly limited to three key defining characteristics: military expertise, responsibility, and what he termed as corporateness. Rejecting the notion of early American military leaders as professionals of any kind, he argues the true military professional is not a "temporary citizen-soldier inspired by intense momentary patriotism and duty" but is devoted to the "permanent desire to perfect himself in the management of violence."[16] Further, unlike the citizen-soldiers and amateurs of the 1700s, the military professional must regard himself as somewhat set apart from the rest of society and operates within a very clearly defined sphere, separate from other jurisdictions. While not a historian, Huntington's contributions to the historical understanding of the state of professionalism in early America were profound and further developed the theme of the sharp distinction between the military professional and the citizen-soldier of the early republic.[17]

In the 1960s, Russell Weigley published two critical works, *Towards an American Army: Military Thought from Washington to Marshall* and *History of the United States Army*, which for the first time provided an academic military historian's interpretation of the nature of early American military professionalism.[18] Weigley carved out a somewhat middle course between Upton and Palmer, arguing that the American military historical experience was "a history of two armies . . . a Regular Army of professional Soldiers and a citizen Army of various components variously known as militia, National Guards, Organized Reserves, selectees."[19] Acknowledging Washington's military preference for regular professionals, Weigley indicates that through experience and extensive training and discipline, both Washington's Continental Army after 1778 and Wayne's Army of 1792-1794 were at least semi-professional armies. In fact, says Weigley, "Wayne deserves to be called the father of the Regular Army for his creation of a well-trained and disciplined army that defeated the Northwest Indians at the battle of Fallen Timbers in 1794."[20] At the same time, Weigley insists that leaders like Washington understood that military effectiveness must be balanced by political concerns over the dangers of militarism resulting from a corruptive standing Army. Weigley rejected Upton's criticisms, arguing that the Prussian model urged by Upton and his adherents was antithetical to the American tradition of strict civilian control of the military and reservations regarding the establishment of an elitist officer corps.[21] Weigley argues that achieving an acceptable balance between trained regulars and militia took considerable time to be established. While he perceived the stirrings of military professionals in the immediate aftermath of the nation's founding, Weigley argued that the regular forces temporarily built by Washington and Wayne in the 1790s were vulnerable and often fell prey to unprofessional influences of partisanship, self-serving greed, and the government's unwillingness (or inability) to consistently provide necessary resources. Thus, he approvingly quotes Winfield Scott's well-known characterization of his fellow officers in the early 1800s as "swaggerers, dependents, decayed gentlemen, and others fit for nothing else."[22]

Following in Weigley's footsteps, historian Edward Coffman also posited a dual American military tradition composed of a smaller regular force of professionals slowly and painfully established in the Revolutionary and post-Revolutionary years as well as a larger body of militia and other non-regular forces. Coffman skillfully describes the way in which these two traditions "have been interwoven with tension and cooperation" from the very beginning of the nation.[23] By the mid-1790s, he argues, there was a growing consensus of the need for a mix of these two traditions and an acceptance that the military establishment needed both a small professional Army and a much larger body of non-regulars. While acknowledging this growing and sometimes grudging acceptance, Coffman also points out the tremendous challenges the regular Army faced before becoming a reliably professional asset: the often catastrophic state of logistical support to the Army and to individual soldiers in terms of food, clothing, equipment and pay; the lack of internal cohesion among the officer corps (often characterized by divisions and even dueling); and a lack of professional focus by leaders distracted by the recurring cycle of draw-downs and build-ups which characterized the regular Army during the years between the Revolution and the War of 1812. Thus, Coffman argued that professionalism developed only after the War of 1812, following transformational reforms in the officer corps.[24]

British historian Marcus Cunliffe was less convinced than Weigley and Coffman that the late 18th century saw military professionalism starting to stir. *In Soldiers and Civilians: The Martial Spirit in America, 1775-1865,* Cunliffe discarded the notion that men such as Washington, Wayne, Nathaniel Greene, or Henry Knox were developing into professionals, calling them "amateur generals" compared to the professional generals they faced in the British Army.[25] Like Huntington, Cunliffe claimed that anti-militarism was dominant in American ideology, restraining any real development of military professionalism until decades after the war of 1812. According to Cunliffe, weak and unreliable militia forces, organizational failure, and chaos caused by recurring draw-downs in the military establishment characterized the first United States Officer Corps. Cunliffe ultimately argued that the dualism in the American military establishment, which he terms civilianness and militarism, is a "problem without a perfect solution" and one which until after the Civil War plagued the United States.[26] Unlike Weigley and Coffman who argued that ultimately this dualism was strength, Cunliffe's writings stress the way this dualism delayed the establishment of consistent American military professionalism. In his view, the American military establishment was dominated by amateurism and politics through the War of 1812. Only in the post-war years would professional officers begin to assert a significant influence. By the 1840s, he argued "the American Regular Army had developed professional styles . . . [and] the principle of professionalism had gained a footing and was not to be dislodged."[27]

Richard Kohn, military historian and author of *The Eagle and Sword: The Federalists and the Creation of the Military Establishment in America, 1783-1802*, expresses overall skepticism about any late 18th century American military professionalism.[28] Kohn emphasizes Washington's influence in forming the early American understanding and practice of military professionalism, arguing that the first president, aided particularly by fellow Federalists Henry Knox and Alexander Hamilton, continually strove throughout the 1790s against the anti-militarist tradition in the young republic in order to create a small "professional army composed of career officers trained in the science of warfare."[29] These efforts, according to Kohn, bore some fruit particularly during General Wayne's campaign against the Northwest Indians, culminating in victory in 1794, but eventually foundered on the shoals of philosophical anti-militarism particularly emphasized by Jeffersonian Republicans, lack of resources necessary to fund a truly professional army, and a lack of a substantial foreign threat warranting a professional force.[30]

One key outcome related to future American military professionalism, according to Kohn, resulted from the centrality of Washington's unswerving devotion to the concept of civilian control of the military. This was most spectacularly demonstrated during Washington's neutralization of the potentially mutinous 1783 Newburgh incident at the end of the Revolutionary War, but Kohn convincingly argues that such a devotion to civilian control was demonstrated by Washington throughout his entire career as military commander and president. This example and influence, says Kohn, was inculcated deeply into the entire American military establishment from the beginning and was accepted from the nation's beginning as the basis of American military professionalism and civil-military relations.[31]

In contrast to Kohn's focus on senior leaders within the American political and military establishments, William Skelton's publication of *An American Profession of Arms: the Army Officer Corps, 1784-1861* marked an attempt to understand the Army not solely through the vision or leadership of senior leaders but through the internal experience within the Army itself.[32] Diving deeply into the lives of officers at all levels of the officer corps, Skelton concludes that the professionalization of the American officer corps occurred in the immediate aftermath of the War of 1812, earlier than had often been accepted by some historians. Skelton argues that the late 18th century Army Officer Corps was defined by instability, heterogeneity, and steady attrition. Thoroughly mining Army records, journals, letters, and memoirs, Skelton provides both an in-depth and sweeping portrait of an officer corps struggling to survive a volatile social and political environment suspicious of military professionalism. Skelton concludes that these factors severely limited military professional development before the War of 1812.[33] After 1815, Skelton argues that professionalism grew quickly, nurtured by a growing practice of lifelong officers educated at West Point, the development of officer cohesion, and public acknowledgement of the need for professional military service.[34]

Other more in-depth works, focusing more specifically on American late 18th century campaigns and the development of the early American Army, provide valuable in-depth discussions. These include Wiley Sword's overview of the Northwest Indian War in his work *President Washington's Indian War, 1790-1795.*[35] *March to Massacre: A History of the First Seven Years of the United States Army, 1784-1791* by William Guthman, convincingly relates the immense struggles of the emerging nation and its military ending in the catastrophes experienced in the Harmar and St. Clair-led campaigns.[36] In *Bayonets in the Wilderness: Anthony Wayne's Legion in the Old Northwest*, Alan Gaff provides a detailed and thorough description and analysis of Anthony Wayne's victorious campaign against the confederation of American Indians in 1794, ending with the battle of Fallen Timbers and the Treaty of Greeneville in 1795. In this work, following the detailed example of Skelton, Gaff deeply describes the internal life of Wayne's Army between 1792 and 1795.[37]

The themes developed by these important scholars in the field of early American military history help to frame this study of the nature of professionalism in the early officers. This study examines the principle themes developed by these scholars. This thesis pays special attention to the enduring themes treated by these scholars, including a focus on the officer corps' response to challenges related to trust, expertise, service, esprit, and stewardship.

Notes

1.   Especially useful in the development of this historiographical essay were historical reviews in Don Higginbotham, "The Early American Way of War: Reconnaissance and Appraisal," *The William and Mary Quarterly* 44, no. 2 (April 1987): 230-273 and Wayne E. Lee, "Early American Ways of War: A New Reconnaissance, 1600-1815," *The Historical Journal* 44, I (2001): 269-289.

2.   Emory Upton, *The Military Policy of the United States* (Washington DC: Government Printing Office, 1904), 16.

3.   Upton, xi, 17.

4.   For varied interpretations of Upton, see Russell Weigley, *Towards an American Army: Military Thought form Washington to Marshall* (New York:. NY Columbia University Press, 1962); Stephen Ambrose, *Upton and the Army* (Baton Rouge, LA: Louisiana University Press, 1964); and David Fitzpatrick's "Emory Upton and the Citizen Soldier" *The Journal of Military History* 65 (April 2001): 355-389.

5.   Quoted in the helpful survey, Don Higginbotham, "American Historians and the Military History of the American Revolution," *The American Historical Review* 70 (October 1964): 18-34.

6.   William Ganoe, *History of the United States Army* (New York, NY: D-Appleton Century Co., 1942); and Trevor Depuy and R. Ernest Depuy, *Military Heritage of America* (New York, NY: McGraw-Hill, 1956).

7.   John McAuley Palmer, *Statesmanship or War* (Garden City, NY: Doubleday, 1927), 74.

8.   John McAuley Palmer, *America in Arms: The Experience of the United States with Military Organization* (New Haven, CT: Yale University Press, 1941).

9.   George Washington, "Sentiments on a Peace Establishment," *The George Washington Papers,* Alderman Library, University of Virginia, Charlottesville, VA, 2 May 1783, http://gwpapers.virginia.edu (accessed 7 May 2013).

10.   George Washington, "Address to the New York Provincial Congress," *The George Washington Papers,* Alderman Library, University of Virginia, Charlottesville, VA, 26 June 1775, http://gwpapers.virginia.edu (accessed 7 May 2013).

11.   On Palmer's scholarship and influence, see Weigley, *Towards an American Army.*

12.   E. Wayne Carp, "The Problem of National Defense in the Early American Republic" in *The American Revolution: Its Character and Limits,* ed. Jack Green (New York, NY: New York University Press, 1987), 18.

13. Samuel Huntington, *The Soldier and the State: The Theory and Politics of Civil-Military Relations* (Cambridge, MA: Belknap Press of Harvard University, 1957).

14. Huntington, 19.

15. Huntington, 226-237.

16. Huntington, 15.

17. On Huntington's influence, see William Skelton, "Samuel P. Huntington and the Roots of the American Military Tradition" *The Journal of Military History* 60 (April, 1996): 325-338.

18. Weigley, *Towards an American Army*; and Russel F. Weigley, *History of the United States Army* (New York, NY: MacMillan, 1967).

19. Weigley, *History of the United States Army*, xi.

20. Weigley, 93.

21. For a good discussion of Weigley's view of Upton and a pro-Upton interpretation, see Fitzpatrick, 355-389.

22. Weigley, *History of the United States Army*, 107.

23. Edward M. Coffman, "The Duality of the American Military Tradition" *Journal of Military History* 64 (October 2000): 969.

24. Edward M. Coffman, *The Old Army: A Portrait of the American Army in Peacetime, 1784-1898* (Oxford, UK: Oxford University Press, 1986); and Coffman, "The Duality of the American Military Tradition: A Commentary," 967-980.

25. Marcus Cunliffe, *Soldiers and Civilians: The Martial Spirit in America, 1775-1865* (Boston, MA: Little and Brown, 1968), 42.

26. Cunliffe, 334.

27. Cunliffe, 149, 151.

28. Richard Kohn, *Eagle and Sword: The Federalists and the Creation of the Military Establishment in America, 1783-1802* (New York, NY: Free Press, 1975).

29. Kohn, 44.

30. Kohn, *Eagle and Sword,* 54.

31. Kohn, 88.

32. William Skelton, *An American Profession of Arms: The Army Officer Corps, 1784-1861* (Lawrence, KS: University of Kansas Press, 1992).

33. Skelton, *An American Profession of Arms:,* 87-88.

34. Skelton, 119.

35. Sword.

36. Guthman.

37. Gaff.

Chapter 3
Military Professionalism and Trust in the Early American Army officer corps, 1789 - 1796

Before discussing the nature of the relationship between military professionalism and trust in the Army officer corps of the early American republic, it may be useful to briefly summarize the key elements of current doctrine concerning this critical relationship. Chapter 2 of *The Army* emphasizes that military professionalism is built upon the concept of trust, which supports the four other essential characteristics of the profession of arms.[1]

Trust is described as the bedrock of professionalism and the "core intangible needed by the Army inside and outside the profession."[2] According to this capstone manual, trust at the most fundamental level relies on the Army being worthy of the faith of the American people that it will always serve the Constitution and nation before all other considerations and thus will not permit the inherent power of a military force to ever threaten constitutional liberty. Absolutely central to the development of this trust is military subordination to civilian authority, by which the Army proves itself a trusted servant of the nation without ulterior or selfish goals.

A second aspect of trust emphasized in the Army's professionalism doctrine concerns trust up and down the chain of command between superiors and subordinates at all levels. This trust is critical to mission effectiveness, stimulating individual and collective commitment to mission accomplishment. Such trust is also required for the effective use of the concept of mission command, the Army's fundamental doctrine for command.

The third aspect of trust involves mutual trust among Soldiers, establishing the unit cohesion necessary to accomplish demanding missions. *The Army* notes that the "level of resilience and cohesion within an Army unit correlates directly to trust between Soldiers in that unit."[3] The fourth and final key aspect of trust described in the Army's doctrine on professionalism is that between the Army and Soldiers and their Families. Such trust is essential to the building of a supportive environment that enhances family strength and resilience.[4]

As in today's doctrine on military professionalism, early leaders of the nation's Army focused on trust as a key element of the military's relationship to society. The building of societal trust in the Army, and particularly the officer corps, was essential because of the wide-spread and significant skepticism in American society that professional armies were compatible with republican liberty. Drawing upon both classical Whig thought and the American pre-Revolutionary experience with British Regulars enforcing curbs on colonial freedom, there was consensus across American society that large European-style professional armies were antithetical to American ideological, political, and social values.[5]

President George Washington, Secretary of War Henry Knox, and the senior military leaders of the new nation understood the critical need to build a military that met both the military and political requirements of the young republic. These leaders turned to a twofold strategy to fashion an effective and trustworthy force. First, the state militias, and not full-time regular forces, were placed at the very heart of the nation's defense establishment.[6] Terming the militia the "great bulwark of our liberties and independence," Washington rejected a large standing Army as too costly in both financial and ideological terms.[7] This prefigured the language used by Knox and Washington in their 1790 proposal for the organization and training of the state militias, arguing, "an energetic national militia is to be regarded as the capital security of a free Republic and not a standing army, forming a distinct class in the community."[8] Finally, such language was consistent with Washington's warning in his presidential farewell address to "avoid the necessity of those overgrown military establishments, which, under any form of government, are inauspicious to liberty and which are to be regarded as particularly hostile to Republican Liberty."[9] Accepting the centrality of militia to the nation's defense, Washington and Knox fought hard to transform the often fickle and undisciplined militia of their Revolutionary War and post-war experience into a more reliable force overseen by federal inspectors with nationally standardized organizations, equipment, and training.[10] Largely unsuccessful in this effort due to financial constraints and jealousy of federal oversight over state militias, some reforms were incorporated into the Militia Law passed in 1792, which provided the framework for militia involvement with the Army for the next century.[11]

The second element of the Washington administration's twofold effort to build an effective military that was compatible with republican ideology, was the building of a small regular Army led by a professional corps of officer deemed acceptable by the American people through an unquestionably trustworthy performance. It is this effort that is the focus of this study, for it was primarily in the small officer corps of the nation's early federal Army that the nature of military professionalism is observable.

The fundamental vehicle by which the Army's leadership sought to build societal trust in the Army was an emphasis on civil-military relations characterized by military subordination to civil authority. Central to this deferential attitude was the respect of the officer corps for the service, stature, and example of the first president. Gordon Wood persuasively argues that Washington's example selflessly subordinating himself and his immediate position to the greater good of American society was of great power and was, in fact, the most important legacy ever left by an American leader.[12] All of the general officers, nearly all of the field grade officers, and some of the junior officers holding such rank in the 1790s during the Washington administration were Revolutionary War veterans and therefore close witnesses of Washington's most striking examples of the subordination of self and Army to the greater good of the new republic.[13] These included his consistent deference to Congressional authority during the Revolution, his voluntary resignation at the conclusion of the war, and his strong refusal during the 1783 Newburgh incident to endanger the principle of military subordination by permitting the Army to subvert civil government.[14]

Washington's influence on the officer corps, including his shaping of their acceptance of military subordination, is indicated by the tremendous affection and respect which pours forth from the letters, journals, and other papers of the officer corps during the early to mid-1790s. In an age of strong opinions and differences among officers, there is a rare near unanimity of thought concerning the Army's commander in chief. Representative of this is Major General Anthony Wayne's recurring allusion to Washington as "that great and good man" whose approbation "has been my constant study and highest ambition," his 1795 confidence in the midst of political strife that "our Great and virtuous President will once more save this country from ruin," and his 1796 praise of Washington's "wisdom and patriotism . . . for which he is so universally and justly celebrated."[15]

The near-universal acceptance of military subordination amidst the officer corps during Washington's presidency is similarly striking, especially given the many military frustrations involved in the Northwest Indian conflict which dominated the work of the American Army during Washington's presidency. Aside from a few anomalous examples, both the official and private papers from Army leaders and officers attest to the full acceptance of the idea that the Army ought to act in selfless accord, in line with the guidance given by the president and his civilian aides, indicating the Army's status as a servant of the American people.[16] All three commanding generals during the Northwest Indian War which include Brevet Brigadier General Josiah Harmar, Major General Arthur St. Clair, and Major General Anthony Wayne, continually sought administration approval for the

Army's major actions and each acquiesced with administration guidance to delay offensive operations pending the results of peace negotiations with hostile Indian tribes despite strident demands from frontier populations for aggressive Army action. Civil-military relations in Wayne's 1792–1794 campaign are particularly revealing of this dynamic. Having been ordered by Washington and Knox to carefully prepare a campaign that would avoid the disasters of the previous two efforts, Wayne spent great effort in 1792 and 1793 preparing logistical support and forward depots in hostile territory to support the Army's planned offensive maneuvers.[17] When Indian leaders engaged in peace negotiations complained of this, citing it as evidence of bad faith negotiating, the administration firmly directed Wayne to cease all such action in forward areas.[18] In response, Wayne candidly laid out the consequences of failing to supply these depots and strongly urged permission to continue logistical preparations, which he saw as necessary for a successful future campaign.[19] When he was still ordered to desist, Wayne respectfully obeyed, fully accepting the concept of civilian control of his Army, asking Knox that "orders may be always as explicit as those . . . (and) I pledge you my honor they shall be obeyed with equal promptitude if in my power."[20]

Fortunately, senior officers' respect for civilian control over the Army during Washington's administration was coupled with the gradual development of a high level of candor and effective communication between the civilian leadership and Army leaders. In examining the correspondence between these leaders, it is evident that the principle of what is today known as mission command, where superiors "trust subordinates and empower them to accomplish missions within their intent" while subordinates respect superiors' guidance and "trust superiors to give them the freedom to execute intent," gradually became a reality during this period.[21]

This development came only after significant struggle. In the 1790 campaign led by General Harmar, the civilian leaders' responsibility to provide strategic direction appeared to be overwhelmed by the crush of other business as the nation's first presidential administration got underway. Washington and Knox appear guilty of allowing the newly named governor of the Northwest Territory, Governor St. Clair, and General Harmar to make operational decisions concerning the use and timing of military force against hostile tribes that undermined the administration's strategic goal of peaceful negotiation with potentially hostile Indian tribes.[22] Throughout the early 1790s, both Washington and Knox insisted that the strategic priority was a negotiated settlement. They argues that, "the best foundation for peace with the Indians is by establishing just and liberal treaties with them" while attempting through diplomacy to cut off British efforts to provoke Indian resistance to American demands.[23]

Unfortunately, both the president and his secretary failed in 1790 to ensure that their subordinates in both the territorial government and the Army devised a plan supportive of this strategy. Despite Knox's original guidance permitting a very limited strike using at most 400 Soldiers to punish a much targeted group of "banditti" for their raids on frontier settlements, St. Clair and Harmar cajoled a reluctant administration into authorizing a far larger and more general mission using a combined Army and a militia force of 1,500 Soldiers.[24] That Washington and Knox allowed "the mantle of deciding war or peace in the Northwest" to fall on Harmar indicates the administration's irresponsibility in allowing a gap between tactical means and strategic ends.[25] Predictably, given this disconnect as well as organizational, training, and leadership deficiencies, the Harmar-led expedition of 1790 ended in military defeat at the hands of the Miami Chief Little Turtle and his confederation of British-supported tribes. Thus, a campaign mounted to deter Indian aggression resulted instead in a far more confident and belligerent confederation of hostile tribes, bent on obstructing further white encroachment on their claimed territory.[26]

Having replaced Harmar with the newly minted Major General Arthur St. Clair, the Washington administration learned from the 1790 error of its ways, providing St. Clair direction that is far more concrete and attempting to better synchronize military and diplomatic efforts. A comparison of the guidance given to Harmar in 1790 and St. Clair in 1791 is evidence of the administration "finally assuming control over its army and all military operations, an elementary procedure that was crucial in the creation of the American military establishment."[27] However, a thorough look at the correspondence between Washington, Knox and St. Clair also reveals a level of inflexibility and one-way communication, as the administration provided firm guidance but neither sought nor particularly welcomed St. Clair's cautions that the Army suffered from a lack of training, organization, and logistical readiness for an offensive. The administration's systematic and firm guidance on the requirement to build a chain of forts along the intended axis of advance, on the application of force and especially on the timing of the offensive indicated a lack of trust in St. Clair's generalship and limited his flexibility and initiative.[28]

In the aftermath of his disastrous defeat by allied tribes again led by Little Turtle and supported by British and Canadian advisors, St. Clair, in that the administration's failure to empower him to use his judgment to determine the timing and details of the offensive, was partially responsible for the defeat. This seems somewhat self-serving in light of the many errors in judgment made by St. Clair and his subordinates. However, given the poor state of training, logistical, and organizational readiness of his force and the administration's determination to execute the campaign before the winter of 1791, St. Clair's complaint of a breakdown in civil-military trust seems justified.[29]

Having swung to opposite extremes during the 1790 and 1791 campaigns, by 1792 the nation's civil and military leaders developed a generally healthy level of trust characterized by a strikingly high degree of candor and respect for each other. Despite the delay in communications caused by an up to eight-week turnaround time for correspondence, Washington, Knox and their new commander, Major General Anthony Wayne, managed to synchronize strategic and tactical ends, ways, and means remarkably well. The free flow of information and respectful seeking and giving of advice, especially when compared to previous civil-military communication, is immediately apparent in the correspondence between these leaders. Washington and Knox focused on synchronizing strategy and military operations, firmly ordering Wayne to delay offensive operations throughout late 1792 and 1793 in order to allow peace negotiations a chance to achieve national goals.[30] At the same time, the administration focused diplomatic efforts in London on splitting the heretofore tightly-allied British and Indian tribes of the Northwest Territory. The administration granted Wayne authorization to initiate offensive operations only when American negotiations with Indian leadership proved unsuccessful in 1793, and when an emerging sense developed that a treaty with Britain was possible, promising British vacating disputed forts on the frontier with a corresponding abandonment of their Indian allies in America. The synchronization of diplomatic and military efforts in 1793 and 1794 indicated an administration capable of learning lessons from the immediate past and a military senior leadership able to function efficiently in an environment conducive to honest and candid civil-military dialogue.[31]

Firmly establishing the broad strategic outline and nesting diplomatic and military operations, the administration entrusted and empowered Wayne with "plenary powers" within the confines of this broad guidance, noting that:

> general ideas have been heretofore pointed out to you, which the Government are desirous of having executed, the practicability of which and the means of accomplishment must be left to your

discretion. Your nearer view of the business will enable you to discover advantages or disadvantages which cannot be perceived at this distance. Your judgment must therefore be confided in . . .[32]

Responding eagerly to such empowerment, Wayne provided Knox and Washington with frequent and detailed recommendations and reports on his Army's training, readiness, and plans coupled with repeated assertions of openness to administration guidance.[33] This led to a steadily increasing level of candor, trust, and transparency even amidst contentious issues. In the aftermath of Wayne's victory at Fallen Timbers in the fall of 1794, the administration's confidence and trust in Wayne rose to new heights, illustrating both the power of success and the current Army doctrinal understanding that "cementing trust depends on fulfilling commitments."[34]

This trust and confidence between the nation's top civil and military leaders continued in the aftermath of Fallen Timbers, resulting in Washington providing broad outlines of his desired strategic direction for negotiations with the defeated Indian confederacy and Wayne being given a significant degree of discretion as the government's senior negotiator.[35] The resulting Treaty of Greeneville, signed in the fall of 1795, was rapidly accepted by the Washington administration and Congress, having achieved nearly all of the stated strategic goals of President Washington.[36]

Closely coupled with the Army's acceptance of civilian control over the military and an emphasis on positive civil-military relations, was a desire throughout the 1790s officer corps to show that the Army was worthy of the trust of the American people and that skeptics' concerns about an Army's tendency to infringe upon free citizens were unwarranted. In constant battle with political foes to maintain both a reliable militia improved by federal oversight and a small and permanent Army, Washington and Knox consistently emphasized the need for the Army to act in such a way as to engender trust by the people. It was especially important in this regard to prove to Americans that the Army served society and thus reflected the requirements and needs of society. Thus, in 1792, Knox reminded Brigadier General James Wilkinson of the difficulty in establishing even a small permanent Army in the United States, noting that in order to mollify republican suspicion that "the seeds of a standing army (were) designed to overturn the liberties of the country," it was necessary that "the Officers, who possess extensive minds must inculcate those principles of economy, obedience to orders, habitual vigilance and sobriety and good morals, so essential to perfect discipline and a dignified military reputation subservient to the Laws."[37] With rare exceptions, the young officer corps during Washington's presidency understood this and fought hard to establish a "good reputation" for the Army among the American people.[38]

This determination is evident in representative actions like that of Captain and Revolutionary War veteran Samuel Newman. Marching his newly formed company west to join the 1791 campaign, the company commander reminded his troops that:

> It is at all times necessary to the Honour, Comfort, and happiness of a Soldier, to conduct himself with decency and good order . . . Any Soldier who may so far forget he is at all times amenable to the Civil Authority, as to wantonly abuse or ill-treat any of the inhabitants of the United States, or is so lost to the Character of a Soldier as to disgrace this detachment by plundering, or Stealing even the smallest article from the Good People of the Country, may depend on being immediately punished on the Spot and that too in a severe and exemplary Manner.[39]

Several weeks later, as his company approached the town of Lancaster, Pennsylvania, Newman ordered his company to halt and to "prepare Clean Shirts, Jackets and Overalls, and to Reserve some of their flour (to powder their hair), that our entrance into the Town may be respectable."[40]

Newman's concern for the Army's reputation and for happy relations between the military and civilians was characteristic of many officers. Garrison orderly books from frontier posts are full of commanders' efforts to limit the impact on civilian communities of disorderly Soldiers' actions.[41] For instance, while serving as commandants at Fort Knox, both Lieutenant Colonel John Francis Hamtramck and Captain Thomas Pasteur ordered and enforced curfews in an attempt to limit complaints from citizens from the nearby town of Vincennes along the Wabash River. When that failed, Pasteur ordered "that the North side of the Street, running East and West by Mrs. Busrones' house to be the limited line between the Garrison and Village, and any Soldier found in any part of the Said Street, or to the South of it, without regular permission, will be deemed Guilty of disobedience of orders, and punished accordingly."[42] Later, Pasteur ordered 100 lashes and reduction in rank for a sergeant who endeavored "to defame the Character of a Young Lady of the Village and for behaving in a seditious manner."[43] That such punishments continued indicate both the challenge of reining in unruly Soldiers and the officers' commitment to building and preserving civilian trust of the Army.

Leaders in the officer corps addressed the perception of Army encroachment on civilian prerogatives very cautiously. Serving as both Northwest Territory Governor and commanding general, St. Clair showed the officer corps' reluctance to impinge on the territory of civilian authority, stating in the aftermath of a local controversy regarding the use of the Army to enforce civil law and to punish infractions that "it is not the business of a military servant of the sovereign authority to take cognizance of breaches of the law, neither has he anything to do with the confinement or release of such persons as may offend therein."[44] Similarly, Anthony Wayne arrived at Fort Pitt in 1792 as the Army's new commander and quickly assured the civilian population of western Pennsylvania that he had neither mandate nor intent to involve the Army in enforcing civilian law, especially the contentious tax on whiskey production. Wayne, with no demurral from the Washington administration, insisted that his Army would not enforce tax collection "for his task was to protect the people and not oppress them."[45] One wonders if the administration appreciated Wayne's choice of words, but it did recognize the threat to civil-military trust posed by the Army's potential involvement in an internal political matter, choosing to instead use the militia to handle the politically sensitive task of quelling the 1794 Whiskey Rebellion.[46]

One final example is also representative of the officer corps' struggle to establish a workable and trustworthy relationship with civilian communities. While commanding the garrison at Fort Washington outside the growing town of Cincinnati, General Wilkinson grew concerned about deteriorating local civil-military relations and restricted Soldiers without permission from the town, on pain of immediate punishment. In May 1792, newly arrived Lieutenant William Henry Harrison and a squad of Soldiers were ordered to conduct a patrol to enforce Wilkinson's restriction and found two artisans (civilian employees of the Army) in town, one of whom was very drunk. Harrison ordered the inebriated artisan whipped on the spot, despite the artisan's protest that he was not subject to military justice. When the other artisan tried to intervene, Harrison ordered him whipped also. The punished artisans accused Harrison of assault and town authorities issued a warrant for Harrison's arrest. Desiring to protect a young officer making a seemingly honest mistake in confusing Soldiers and civilian employees, Wilkinson lightly reprimanded Harrison but refused entry to the fort for local authorities bent on arresting Harrison. At the same time, Wilkinson understood the need to placate the frustrated civilian authorities and thus clarified his order, exempting civilian employees both from his order and from the application of military justice. When this failed to appease the local judge and sheriff who promised to arrest Harrison the moment he entered Cincinnati, Wilkinson craftily sent Harrison to Philadelphia, to escort Wilkinson's wife in her travels there and as courier carrying papers to the War Department. This seemed to solve the issue. When the lieutenant returned to Fort Washington during preparations for the 1794 campaign, local authorities no longer sought his apprehension.[47]

By 1794, it is clear that the young republic's leaders had established generally positive and professional civil-military relations concerning the shared pursuit of national and military missions and the Army's selfless commitment to "putting the nation first, above all other considerations."[48] Other aspects of the civil-military relationship however, were neither so positive nor so encouraging to the development of a professional officer corps. Specifically, political and financial tensions within the nation led to a significant lack of stability within the Army and particularly in the officer corps. This instability greatly impeded the development of trust among officers that the country valued professional military officership. Emerging partisanship and political party development, continuing skepticism about the compatibility of a professional officer corps leading a standing Army, and the continuing financial weakness of the young nation resulted in recurring efforts in Congress to weaken the regular Army. Wayne's admonition to Knox regarding this situation was ominous, warning in early 1793 that Congressional attempts to decrease the size of the Army and the officer corps resulted in officers perceiving "that they hold their Commissions on a very precarious tenor," which "has had a very visible and injurious effect upon the minds of the Officers, many of whom have already resigned and others are determined to follow their example, and therefore feel neither interest or pride in the discipline or appearance of their men."[49]

While significant force structure cuts were largely avoided during Washington's presidency, recurring attempts by Congress to reduce the Army took a serious toll on the Army officer corps. In particular, these attempts undermined the officers' trust that Congress and the American people understood what *The Army* refers to as the need among Soldiers for society to remember the sacrifice of Soldiers, "with respect and appreciation for having done their duty."[50] The damaging impact of instability and the related perceived lack of societal appreciation introduced a hint of resentment into the officer corps.[51] Harmar, writing sarcastically to Major Hamtramck in 1789, reminded his subordinate and Fort Knox Commander to adhere to the requirement to send detailed rosters four times a year as "these frequent musters will serve to refresh the memory of government, and to let them know that they have a regiment upon the frontiers."[52] In late 1795, Lieutenant William Clark complained to his brother "the army has become disagreeable to me and could I get into any business in a civil capacity I would bid adieu to this unthankful unpolish'd service."[53] The timing of this assertion, made at the height of political attempts to cut the size and influence of the regular Army, and the reference to a lack of thanks for his service makes it likely that Clark resented the instability of the young Army. Similarly, Lieutenant William H. Harrison was dismayed by rumors in 1796 that the Army officer corps would be cut in half and angrily submitted his letter of resignation, explaining that "the very illiberal treatment which I have met with from the government has determined me to abandon the profession of arms entirely in a short time."[54] Wayne managed to deter the promising and well-connected captain from immediate resignation but Harrison began searching for alternate opportunities and when the position of Northwest Territory Secretary opened, Harrison resigned his commission and took up his new station.[55]

Such feelings of resentment were tempered in the 1790s by periods of strong societal appreciation for the Army. Unsurprisingly, this was especially true in moments when communities perceived an urgent need for protection from threats or in the aftermath of victory. Thus in 1793, with frontier settlements dismayed by two unsuccessful campaigns and suffering increasing Indian raids, Army officers remarked with great satisfaction the boisterous welcome by citizens of Cincinnati when the Legion arrived to begin offensive operations against hostile tribes. Similarly, Philadelphia society welcomed Anthony Wayne and his officers home from the successful Fallen Timbers campaign with honorary cavalry escorts, artillery salutes, parades, and multiple dinners in honor of Wayne and his victorious Army.[56]

The next discussion regarding trust and professionalism in *The Army* involves trust between Soldiers. The tendency for the characteristics of professionalism to overlap in the Army's current doctrine on professionalism is especially pronounced here, as the importance of trust between Soldiers is emphasized in both the sections on trust and on esprit. This thesis discusses such trust in the later chapter on esprit, as it seems to better fit the doctrinal emphasis on the intimate connection between esprit, cohesion, teamwork and trust within the Army.[57]

The final element of trust as described in *The Army*, involves the relationship between Soldiers and their families with the Army. It is in this area that, by current standards, the Army of the 1790s failed most decisively. There was neither the political will nor the financial resources to consistently provide a supportive environment that enhanced "familial strength and resilience.[58] The intensity of the 1780s opposition to the granting of promised half-pay to Revolutionary War officers is indicative of society's unease with the idea of wholeheartedly endorsing the modern concept of military professionals trading expertise and service for financial and societal benefits. Neither society, government, nor the institutional Army was necessarily uncaring about family needs as efforts were made to care for families in difficult situations. In 1794, having experienced a significant number of killed or wounded officers, Congress did enact half-pay pensions for widows of officers killed in action and a stipend for families of disabled veteran officers.[59] Discipline was sometimes enforced against Soldiers who failed to support their families, with Wayne directing that payment and rations of Soldiers not in compliance with this requirement go directly to their dependents.[60]

Aside from cases involving catastrophic loss or disability, the basic idea of a family covenant as understood in current doctrine concerning families and trust was relatively unfamiliar. This was not unique to the Army; late eighteenth century American society appears not to have consistently recognized modern day expectations for an environment especially supportive of family cohesion and resilience.

In conclusion, during the early 1790s, the Washington administration developed a holistic approach to the nation's defense establishment which attempted to meet both the political and military needs of the young republic. The president and his aides, with only partial success, sought to form a strong and reliable militia reformed by federal oversight and standardized organization, equipment, and training. Simultaneous with this effort, Washington and Knox, in coordination with the Army's senior leaders, attempted to build a small and permanent force led by professional officers committed to selflessly serving the nation and earning the trust of an American society prone to view military professionalism with some degree of skepticism. In the course of the development of this latter force, the Army's commanding officers developed strong civil-military relationships with the executive branch, characterized in 1792 by a full acceptance of the notion of military subordination to civil authority, by vigorous and productive interplay and dialogue between senior civil-military leaders, and by a determination among Army officers to earn civilian society's respect and trust. At the same time, the officer corps struggled with building trusting relationships internal to the officer corps. This is examined at length in a later chapter. Finally, neither the political nor the military leadership of the 1790s military could reasonably be expected to transcend the age and focus on a modern and covenantal-type trust between serving families and the Army.

Simultaneous to the struggle to build trusting relationships as professional officers, the Army officer corps of the early 1790s sought to foster the development of military expertise which is the subject of the next chapter. The integration of trust with military expertise was at the heart of the challenge to develop a professional American officer corps.

Notes

1. This summary is drawn from Headquarters, Department of the Army, ADP 1, ch. 2; Headquarters, Department of the Army, *Whitepaper - Our Army Profession* (Draft) (Washington, DC: Government Printing Office, 24 March 2012), 3; training support literature in Headquarters, Army Training and Doctrine Command, *America's Army*, 9.

2. Headquarters, Department of the Army, ADP 1, sect. 2-1.

3. Headquarters, Department of the Army, ADP 1, sect. 2-2.

4. ADP 1, sect. 2-7.

5. The two most insightful and balanced descriptions of the influence of classical Whig thought concerning the troubled relationship between republicanism and professional militaries and American responses to this tension are Lawrence D. Cress, *Citizens in Arms: The Army and the Militia in American Society to the War of 1812* (Chapel Hill, NC: University of North Carolina Press, 1982) and Don Higginbotham, *George Washington and the American Military Tradition* (Athens, GA: University of Georgia Press, 1985).

6. Influential historical works like the posthumous Upton, *The Military Policy of the United States* and Kohn, *Eagle and Sword* argue that Washington and Knox sought to build as large a permanent force as politically possible but historians like Cress and Higginbotham (see footnote five above) better understand that while President Washington and aides like Knox certainly fought for a permanent force to counter threats to the frontier and seaboard and wanted a professional establishment, their desired regular force was always strictly limited, especially compared to the militia.

7. Washington, "Sentiments on a Peace Establishment," published in May 1783 after a request for his views on the Confederation's military need, shows an early consistency to his presidential acceptance of the militia as the primary mechanism for national defense.

8. Knox's Militia Act of 1790 proposal, approved by Washington and sent to Congress. United States, *American State Papers, Military Affairs*, 7.

9. George Washington, "Farewell Address," *The George Washington Papers,* Alderman Library, University of Virginia, Charlottesville, VA, 26 September 1796, http://gwpapers.virginia.edu (accessed 7 May 2013).

10. This is what both Washington's plan, expressed in his "Sentiments on a Peace Establishment," and the administration's 1790 Militia Act proposal advocated.

11. Especially helpful in describing administration attempts to establish a more stable and better organized and trained militia are Kohn, *Eagle and Sword* and Ward, *The Department of War*.

12. Gordon S. Wood makes this argument in the essay "The Greatness of George Washington," in Don Higginbotham, ed., *George Washington Reconsidered* (Charlottesville, VA: University of Virginia Press, 2001), 309-324.

13. The primary source for biographical data on officers in the 1790s is Heitman.

14. Higginbotham, *George Washington and the American Military Tradition*, 69-105.

15. Knopf, *Anthony Wayne*, Wayne to Knox, 7 May 1794, 322; Knopf, *Anthony Wayne,* Wayne to Secretary of War Thomas Pickering, 9 August 1795, 442; and Paul D. Nelson, *Anthony Wayne: Soldier of the Early Republic* (Bloomington, IN: Indiana University Press, 1985), Wayne to Major William Winston, 5 September 1796, 297. In addition, respect for Washington is evident in the annual boisterous celebrations at multiple frontier posts of the president's birthday in Knopf, Anthony Wayne, Wayne to Knox, 22 February 1793, 192.

16. Specific examples are cited in the following text of this thesis and analogous footnotes, but correspondence between the War Department and all three of the commanders of the Army during this period – Harmar, St. Clair and Wayne – reveal the full acceptance of military deference to executive office strategic guidance. The one glaring example of a kind of military insubordination from senior Army leaders was the conduct of Brigadier General James Wilkinson. His case and influence is discussed later in this thesis but his treasonous actions as a secret Spanish agent while serving as the second ranking regular Army general under Wayne were not conducive to the establishment of healthy civil-military relations, but were an anomaly in the general pattern.

17. Knopf, *Anthony Wayne*, Wayne to Knox, 27 May 1793, 242.

18. Knopf, Knox to Wayne, 20 July 1793, 256-257.

19. Knopf., Wayne to Knox, 27 April 1793, 228-230.

20. Knopf, *Anthony Wayne*, Wayne to Knox, 8 August 1793, 265.

21. This description of mission command comes from the Headquarters, Department of the Army, *Whitepaper - Our Army Profession,* 5.

22. Primary source evidence found in correspondence between Harmar, St. Clair, Knox and Washington supports Richard Kohn's claim that in 1790 "military strategy now controlled the Indian policy which it was supposed to serve." Kohn, *Eagle and Sword*, 104.

23. Thornbrough, *Outpost on the Wabash,* Knox to Harmar, 19 December 1889, 211.

24. United States, *American State Papers, Indian Affairs*, Knox to Harmar, 24 August 1790, 99; and William Smith, *St. Clair Papers*, Knox to St. Clair, 23 August 1790, 162.

25. Ward, *The Department of War,* 107.

26. Sword, *President Washington's Indian War* provides a good overview of Harmar's campaign and the negative results.

27. Kohn, *Eagle and Sword*, 111.

28. William Smith, *St. Clair Papers*, Knox to St. Clair, 25 August 1791, 232.

29. These claims were made during the Congressional inquiry into the defeat and published in United States, *American State Papers, Military Affairs*, 36-39, as well as in Arthur St. Clair, *A Narrative of the Manner in Which the Campaign Against the Indians, in the Year One Thousand, Seven Hundred and Ninety one, Was Conducted, Under the Command of Major-General St. Clair* (Philadelphia, PA: Jane Aitken, 1812).

30. Knopf, *Anthony Wayne*, Knox to Wayne, 20 July 1793, 256-257.

31. Sword, *President Washington's Indian War,* and Kohn, *Eagle and Sword* are persuasive that the Washington administration and senior Army leaders greatly improved their performance between 1789 and 1794, synchronizing elements of national power and diplomacy to achieve strategic goals.

32. Knopf, *Anthony Wayne*, Knox to Wayne, 17 May 1793, 239.

33. Knopf, *Anthony Wayne,* 27 April 1793, 230.

34. Headquarters, Department of the Army, *Whitepaper - Our Army Profession,* 5.

35. Knopf, *Anthony Wayne*, 8 April 1795, 393-407.

36. Knopf., Pickering to Wayne, 3 October 1795, 462-463.

37. Ward, *The Department of War,* Knox to Wilkinson, 17 July 1792, 147.

38. This was a difficult mission, for the enlisted Soldiers of the 1790s Army were often quite disorderly with a great affection for alcohol, as is quickly evident in an examination of the period's order and garrison book. The tendency toward disorder among 1790s Soldiers is also well-documented in James Ripley Jacobs, *The Beginning of the US Army, 1783-1812* (Princeton, NJ: Princeton University Press, 1947) and Coffman, *The Old Army*.

39. Samuel Newman, "A Picture of the First United States Army: The Journal of Captain Samuel Newman," ed. Milo M. Quaife, *Wisconsin Magazine of History* 2 (September 1918): journal entry of 31 July 1791, 44. Newman was later killed in the campaign.

40. Newman, Journal entry of 3 August 1791, 46.

41. Especially valuable for providing insight into civil-military relations in garrison environments are Newman; Richard C. Knopf, ed., *A Surgeon's Mate at Fort Defiance: The Journal of Joseph Gardner Andrews for the Year 1795* (Columbus, OH: Ohio Historical Society, 1957); and Consul W butterfield, ed., *Journal of Capt. Jonathan Heart on the March with His Company from Connecticut to Fort Pitt, in Pittsburgh, Pennsylvania, from the Seventh of September, to the Twelfth of October, 1785* (Albany, NY: J. Munsell's Sons, 1885).

42. Newman, 31 December 1795 entry, 157.

43. Newman., 19 April 1796 entry, 162.

44. Smith, *St. Clair Papers,* St. Clair to Judge Turner, 19 June 1791, 218.

45. Nelson, *Anthony Wayne*, Wayne to Knox, 15 June 1792, 228.

46. Washington insisted on the need for a very sensitive approach to this revolt, carefully selecting militia units considered to be both reliable and less inflammatory to the rebels, while at the same time ordering officers commanding the militia marching to western Pennsylvania to quiet the revolt to operate with a light and disciplined hand in order to limit civilian harm or local outrage. See for instance, George Washington, "Washington's Guidance to General Henry Lee," *George Washington Papers,* Alderman Library, University of Virginia, Charlottesville, VA, 20 October 1794, http://rotunda. upress.virginia.edu/founders/GEWN (accessed 7 May 2013). This again indicates Washington's constant desire to build civilian trust not just of the regular Army but also of militia forces.

47. This incident is most fully described in a biography of the young William Henry Harrison in Hendrik Booraem, *A Child of the Revolution: William Henry Harrison and His World, 1773-1798* (Kent, OH: Kent State University Press, 2012), 94-96.

48. Headquarters, Department of the Army, *Whitepaper - Our Army Profession,* 2.

49. Knopf, *Anthony Wayne*, Wayne to Knox, 15 January 1793, 171.

50. Headquarters, Department of the Army, ADP 1, sect. 2-7.

51. This limited but real sense of estrangement was not new to the early republic; as Charles Royster, *A Revolutionary People at War* (Chapel Hill, NC: University of North Carolina Press, 1979) argues convincingly, the Continental Army during the Revolutionary War developed a sense of resentment toward civilians often seen by the Army as indifferent to the sacrificial service of devoted patriot-Soldiers.

52. Thornbrough, *Outpost on the Wabash,* Harmar to Hamtramck, 15 February 1789, 155.

53. Landon Y. Jones, *William Clark and the Shaping of the West* (New York, NY: Hill and Wang, 2004), Clark to Jonathon Clark, 25 November 1794, 81.

54. Booraem, Harrison to Wayne, 11 July 1796, 163.

55. Booraem, 164-165.

56. Wayne and his fellow officers' homecoming is described in Nelson, *Anthony Wayne*, 240, 287-288.

57. Headquarters, Department of the Army, ADP 1, sect. 2-23.

58. ADP 1, sect. 2-25.

59. Coffman, *Old Army*, 37-38.

60. Knopf, *Orderly Books of the United States Legion,* 43.

Chapter 4
Military Professionalism and Military Expertise in the Early
American Army Officer Corps, 1789 – 1796

Following *The Army's* description of trust and its relationship to military professionalism, the capstone manual turns to the principle of military expertise, which it defines as the employment of "a high level of skill in applying knowledge in actual situations."[1]

Professionalism, according to this 2012 doctrine, requires knowledge gained and maintained across four broad fields. Military-technical knowledge involves a doctrinal understanding of the Army's use of landpower, including the organization of units, the planning and execution of operations, and the use and adaptation of technology. Moral-ethical knowledge provides an awareness of the relationship between military force and moral, ethical and legal concerns. Political-cultural understanding discerns the interplay between effective operations of Soldiers and units in relation to the larger society, including both foreign and domestic groups and institutions. Finally, leader development and knowledge are intimately linked, with ongoing education ensuring that military professionals possess the unique knowledge required to provide dynamic leadership in a military environment.[2] The application of knowledge is most effectively done in an environment emphasizing the concept of mission command, in which "competent leaders apply their expertise to the situation as it exists on the ground and accomplish the mission based on their commander's intent."[3]

This chapter considers the nature of the expertise of the early American officer corps in light of these general themes concerning professionalism. First, this chapter examines the nature of the development of military knowledge in the officer corps, including a look at both the type of knowledge sought and the manner knowledge was imparted. Second, it turns to a discussion of the way in which military knowledge was applied with a focus on the three critical actions involving the American Army during this time period, those of the 1790, 1791, and the 1792-1794 campaigns against hostile tribes north of the Ohio River.

The lack of any formal system of military education is one of the striking characteristics of the American Army during its formative years. In the 1790s, officers received no formal schooling either prior to or after commissioning. The experience of new officers like Ensign William Henry Harrison is representative of the lack of any formal education in the 1790s Army. The 18-year-old Harrison sought and earned a commission in August 1791 without any previous exposure to the military, aided by his family connections and the influence of Governor Richard Henry Lee, a confidante of Washington.[4] The lack of any preparation must have been at least slightly jarring to Harrison, as he later wrote that after requesting his commission through Lee, "in twenty four hours . . . I was an ensign in the 1st U. S. Regt of Infantry."[5] Harrison, like nearly all other newly commissioned officers, received no officer training but undertook recruiting duty immediately after commissioning.[6]

The lack of any institutional forum for leader education was not a result of any dismissal of the importance of military knowledge by Army leaders themselves. Senior leaders like President Washington and Secretary Knox had a long record appreciating the value of formal military schooling for officers. During the Revolution, Knox spearheaded the 1778 establishment of a winter-camp academy at Pluckemin, New Jersey for artillery officers, which in addition to artillery-focused topics, taught "battle tactics and logistics, military principles, the considerations a commander had to make before engaging the enemy, (and) the common errors and traps that officers fell into on the battlefield."[7] Washington insisted again and again in the post-Revolution period on the need for formal military schooling, culminating with his urge in a farewell address to Congress in 1796 that the "art of war is at once comprehensive and complicated, that it demands much previous study, and that the possession of it in its most improved and perfect state is always of great moment to the security of a nation. This, therefore, ought to be a serious care of every government, and for this purpose an academy where a regular course of instruction is given is an obvious expedient . . ."[8]

Washington's sense of the value of formal schooling for young officers is evident in his acquiescing to Senator Ralph Izard's request for a commission for his son George Izard in 1794 and the president's advice that the best way to prepare the 18-year-old for military service was to "send him to France and place him in a school of engineers" at Metz commonly attended by French military officers.[9] Thus, on the advice of Washington (though through the financial support of his family), between 1795 and 1797, Lieutenant Izard studied alongside French officers, likely the first newly commissioned American officer in the new republic to receive formal military education.[10]

In 1795, Washington and Knox established a school at West Point for the military education of officers assigned to the Army's Corps of Artillerists and Engineers, newly formed in 1794. Three French officers - Lieutenant Colonel and Commandant Stephen Rochefontaine, Major J. Ulrich Rivardi, and Major Louis Tousard – were commissioned to establish and teach officers the basics of artillery and military engineering. While some education took place, personal rivalry among the French officers, resistance to the foreign instructors, lack of financial support spurred by continued Congressional ideological opposition, and the need for officers to garrison frontier posts vacated by the British, led to the end of the short-lived school at West Point by 1797.[11]

Appreciation for the importance of formal military schooling was not limited to civilian Army leadership. The example of Henry Burbeck illustrates this point. A veteran of the Revolutionary War during which he served as an officer in Knox's Artillery, Captain Burbeck rejoined the Army in 1786 and served as the commander of the West Point garrison from 1787 to 1789. During his command, he unsuccessfully urged the government to immediately create a military academy at West Point. Following service on the southwest frontier, Major Burbeck led Wayne's artillery in the Fallen Timbers campaign from 1792 to 1794, followed by command of Fort Mackinac on the Great Lakes from 1796 to 1799.[12]

It is obvious that Lieutenant Colonel Burbeck continued his earlier interest in military schooling for in 1800, newly promoted to the command of the Army's corps of artillery and engineers, he submitted a proposal to Secretary of War Samuel Dexter, outlining his recommendation for a "Military School, for instructing the arts of gunnery, fortifications, pyrotechny, and everything relative to the art of war."[13] In 1801, temporarily unsuccessful in this attempt, Burbeck outlined his plan to his long-time friend and fellow Revolutionary veteran, the new Secretary of War Henry Dearborn. With the approval of a modified plan for the creation of an academy at West Point, Colonel Burbeck, now commandant of the re-organized Army's regiment of artillery, continued to play a vital role in its establishment, directing operations through subordinates like Lieutenant Colonel Tousard and Major Jonathon Williams. In the eyes of one scholar, Burbeck "may justly be regarded as the founder of the United States Military Academy."[14] While an overstatement, such claims do show Burbeck's commitment to the vision of Washington and Knox and reveal that an understanding of the need for formal military education developed within the officer corps and ultimately supported the creation of the United States Military Academy at West Point in 1802.

While leaders like Washington, Knox, and Burbeck thus clearly valued formal military education, financial weaknesses and ideological concerns prevented any such significant development until the next decade. Some influential scholars like Samuel Huntington and Alan Millett draw upon this fact in arguing that military professionalism in the American Army only developed in the latter half of the nineteenth century, as educational institutions like West Point and the School of Application for Infantry and Cavalry at Fort Leavenworth (forerunner to today's Command and General Staff College) increasingly focused military professionals on the theory of war.[15] But these scholars fail to recognize that leaders of the early Army possessed other means by which the desired and necessary military knowledge could be developed. The two primary means utilized by the early officer corps to develop knowledge were self-development through reading and by leveraging military experience. This mirrored conventional eighteenth century patterns of skilled vocational development, which relied on individual study often coupled with an apprentice type experience or on the job training.[16]

The existence and use of Frederick William Baron Von Steuben's *Regulations for the Order and Discipline of the Troops of the United States*, popularly known as the Blue Book because of the blue material with which it was commonly bound, was critical to the development of standardized military knowledge among officers. Originally published at the request of Washington and approved by Congress in 1779, this manual is often mistaken for a simple manual of drill but it was far more. Divided into 25 chapters, the regulation contains eight chapters focused on drill, seven chapters on platoon, company, battalion, and regimental offensive and defensive maneuvers as well as the use of artillery and cavalry, six chapters on camp discipline and order, and ends with four chapters on specific leader responsibilities, ranging from the regimental commander down to the newly minted ensign.[17] Heavily focused on officer duties, the regulation included practical guidance like a detailed description of overseeing sentry operations as well as more general counsel. For instance, the manual directed that the company commander must "pay the greatest attention to the health of his men, their discipline, arms, accoutrements, ammunition, clothes and necessaries."[18]

In an Army officer corps devoid of any formal educational system, the Blue Book was relied upon heavily by Army leaders; as Walter Kretchik convincingly argues, it became the Army's foundational doctrine for the 1790s officer corps.[19] Brevet Brigadier General Josiah Harmar carried his own copy throughout his 1790 campaign, while consistently directing his officers' attention to Steuben's *Regulations*.[20] In 1792, Major General Anthony Wayne expressed dismay at the lack of available copies for his new officers and asked and received enough copies of the Blue Book and the Army's Articles of War for all of the Army's officers.[21] Wayne's campaign in particular reveals the use of the *Regulations* to standardize camp order, discipline, and training.[22] Of course, it is difficult to know how extensively the available *Regulations* was used by more junior officers, though there are indications that by 1792, younger officers also accepted the fundamental importance of the early doctrine. On Christmas day in 1792, Ensign Hugh Brady performed his first duty as an officer overseeing the Army's picket guard. In his memoirs, Brady wrote of this first duty that "I had Baron Steuben's Tactics, and a good old sergeant, and was pretty well prepared to receive the rounds (of more senior officers) when they approached."[23] Ensign Harrison reported that he spent much of his time as a brand new officer studying the Blue Book, in addition to other martial literature.[24] During the Lewis and Clark expedition the following decade, Captain William Clark and Captain Meriwether Lewis employed Steuben's directions in ordering camp life and establishing guards, having learning these guiding principles during their service as junior officers under Wayne in the mid-1790s.[25]

Washington and Knox, by personal example and in their direction to subordinates, emphasized the importance of self-development through further individual military reading. Washington was convinced of the importance of such reading for military expertise, consistently urging this practice on his officers from the 1750s as a young colonel of Virginia forces to his time as commanding general during the Revolution.[26] Knox, a pre-Revolution owner of a book shop in Boston, was well-known for his intensive study on the art and science of war which led in part to his rapid rise to command the Army's artillery in the Revolution.[27]

All three commanding generals of the Army during Washington's presidency were committed to self-development in military expertise through studying military literature. In the late 1780s, General Harmar was reported to have studied "European treatises" on regimental operations, envisioning his small force as a regiment.[28] During his 1790 campaign, he referenced the writings of Lieutenant Colonel Henry Bouquet, a successful British officer in the French and Indian War, and evidently adjusted his plans to accord with Bouquet's counsel on adapting standard European practices to forest warfare.[29] General Arthur St. Clair and General James Wilkinson shared multiple volumes on military theory and application, including Julius Caesar's *Commentaries* and Lancelot Turpin de Crisse's *Essay on the Art of War*.[30] General Wayne, according to his biographer, "devoured every piece of martial literature he could lay his hands on," paying special attention to Marshal Maurice Saxe's *Reveries upon the Art of War* and Caesar's *Gallic Wars*."[31] Wayne often referenced these favorites in explaining his approach to both leadership and operations, once writing to Washington that he modeled operations after the example of "Caesar at Amiens (and) at Alesia," and citing the power of surprise which "Marshal Saxe Justly Observes proceeds from the Consternation which is the Unavoidable effect of Sudden and unexpected Events."[32]

It is uncertain how seriously more junior officers reflected the example and counsel of the Army's senior leaders and focused on individual self-development through reading. A survey of available journals and diaries of these officers indicates that at least several availed themselves of military histories, theory, and tactics, but in a majority of these primary sources, there is no record of such self-study.[33]

It is clear that senior Army leaders and field grade officers during Washington's presidency possessed a vast amount of military experience, which they perceived to be the foundation for military expertise. Along with character, Washington and his cabinet considered military experience to be of the utmost significance in the selection of the Army's senior leaders. Washington asked St. Clair to take command of the Army in 1791, citing the latter's knowledge of the frontier and his Revolutionary War experience as a senior leader. Similarly in 1792, the president selected Wayne for command of the Army based on his experience as a commander against the British, and due to his acceptability to a wide swath of political leaders.[34] A brief survey of all three of the Army's commanding generals during Washington's presidency reveals extensive military experience.

Pennsylvanian Josiah Harmar, while least prominent of the three commanders of the Army during this period, was an experienced veteran. Entering the officer corps as a captain in 1775, Harmar rose to the rank of lieutenant colonel in the Revolution, seeing action as a regimental commander and staff officer in many of the war's leading campaigns. Influenced by Washington's recommendation and his state's leading role in furnishing troops to the miniscule Army, in 1784 the Confederation Congress chose Harmar to command the existing 700-man force. In this role, he served as the Army's senior commander and as a brevet brigadier general through the 1790 campaign.[35]

Arthur St. Clair was an even more experienced veteran. A native of Scotland, he served five years as a junior officer in the British Army's Royal American Regiment during the French and Indian War, taking part in the 1758 Nova Scotia offensive and in the 1759 battle for Quebec. Resigning his commission in 1762, St. Clair settled in Pennsylvania. With the outbreak of war in 1775, St. Clair took sides with his adopted land and received a commission as colonel. Participating in most of the major campaigns of the war as a commander of a regiment and later of the Pennsylvania Line, he rose to major general by 1783. Leaving the Army at the end of the war to serve in senior civil positions culminating in his appointment as Governor of the Northwest Territory, St. Clair was called back by Washington in 1791 as the Army's commanding general in the aftermath of Harmar's unsuccessful campaign.[36]

Anthony Wayne also served throughout the Revolution, joining the Continental Army as a lieutenant colonel. Serving as a commander of a Pennsylvania regiment, the Continental Corps of Light Infantry, and the Pennsylvania Line, Wayne fought in most of the war's major campaigns and ended the war in 1783 as a major general. Washington recalled him to active service as a major general, replacing St. Clair after his disastrous defeat along the Wabash in 1791. Wayne served as the Army's senior officer from 1792 until his death in late 1796.[37]

Like their three commanders, the Army's field grade officers were experienced officers. Of 39 field grade officers identified as serving in the regular Army between 1789 and 1796, 36 were Revolutionary War veterans, most with extensive and lengthy combat service as officers. All of the regular officers serving as field grade commanders under Harmar, St. Clair, and Wayne possessed significant Revolutionary War experience. A significant minority of captains serving from 1789 to 1796 were also veterans of the Revolution.[38]

Junior officers without such combat experience were expected to rapidly gain experience by active duty, described by Wayne as a new officer's "Military school."[39] One of the most striking characteristics of the acquisition of experience by junior officers during this time is the broadness of quickly-earned experiences within the officer corps. This indicates several essential elements of the nature of military expertise in the early American officer corps. First, military officers were expected to possess knowledge and competence in a very wide-ranging number of activities including, in addition to combat operations, recruitment of Soldiers, diplomacy with tribal leaders, fortification construction, exploration, civil government administration in the absence of civil institutions, and foreign government liaison. Such a breadth of duties clearly indicates a belief among Army leaders that officers required the broad military, technical, political, and cultural knowledge referenced in current doctrine, as articulated by today's *The Army*. Second, officers were expected to rapidly gain knowledge and expertise, often being given significant levels of responsibility and autonomy in executing critical missions. Several representative examples illustrate these characteristics that were repeated again and again in the experiences of officers between 1789 and 1796. These examples are framed by a description of Lieutenant William Clark's representative activities as an officer in Wayne's Legion.

Already a veteran of three punitive militia raids across the Ohio River in 1789 and 1791, Clark gained a federal Army commission in early 1792. The 21-year-old officer spent the summer near his home in Kentucky, seeking to fill his quota of 30 enlisted recruits for Wayne's newly organized Legion. In November of 1792, Clark was ordered to lead a detachment carrying military supplies via the Ohio and Wabash Rivers 375 miles from Fort Steuben near present day Louisville to Fort Knox, near present day Vincennes, Indiana. The rivers having frozen shortly after his arrival at Fort Knox, Clark safely led his detachment overland back through territory dominated by hostile Indians.[40] Junior officers were commonly sent off on such long-range expeditions, often through and by hostile territory, to supply the far-flung forts that marked the 1790s frontier.[41]

Once back at Fort Steuben, Clark was directed from Fort Washington to the mouth of the Kentucky River to build a small fort for defense of river travel and as a depositary for corn for the Army. Responsible for selecting the construction site and designing and overseeing his Soldiers' construction of several blockhouses, a storage barn, and a stockade, Clark completed the duty in one month.[42] Fortification construction was a common duty for the young Army and the design and oversight fell to the officer corps. The Army constructed Fort Washington in 1790, Fort Hamilton and Fort Jefferson in 1791, Fort Greeneville and Fort Recovery in 1793, and Fort Defiance and Fort Wayne in 1794, in addition to numerous smaller blockhouses along the area's river network. General St. Clair's detailed description of the construction of Fort Hamilton illustrates the amount of design and work required to build such wilderness forts, including clearing the ground, building a fifty-yard wide stockade, four bastions with platforms for artillery, a guard house, a store house, and a barracks each for enlisted men and officers.[43] Recognizing the challenge such construction offered, Harmar commended the "indefatigable industry and attention" of Captain William Ferguson and Lieutenant John Pratt in overseeing the 1790 construction of Fort Washington.[44]

Having completed the construction of the riverside blockhouse in the spring of 1793, Lieutenant Clark received summer-time orders from Wayne to lead a detachment of 24 men and three armed flatboats filled with corn, weapons and other goods from Fort Washington down the Ohio and Mississippi Rivers to deliver materials promised by treaty to friendly Chickasaw Indians near present day Memphis, Tennessee. Traveling at night to avoid Spanish posts along the Mississippi that might be tempted to seize the valuable cargo, Clark successfully delivered his goods and managed to recruit nine Chickasaw scouts for the Legion, returning overland along the Natchez Trace.[45] This earned Wayne's attention, noting to Knox that Clark "executed his orders . . . with a promptitude & address that does him honor & which merits my highest appropriation!"[46]

In 1795, Clark was again dispatched by barge with a small detachment on a diplomatic mission, this time to demand the vacating of a Spanish outpost encroaching on the eastern (American) side of the Mississippi River at Chickasaw Bluffs. After delivering his message to the Spanish commandant, Clark brought his men back overland. En route, he demonstrated his hunting prowess by killing 11 bears in one nine-day period to supply his small party![47]

Such diplomatic missions were commonly directed toward officers of the young Army. Missions to potentially hostile Indian tribes were especially risky; Major Alexander Trueman bravely volunteered to act as an emissary to the Miami tribes in 1792, but demonstrating a stunning naivety regarding the Indian threat, was killed by hostile Miami warriors after agreeing to tie up his servant at night to demonstrate friendly intentions.[48] In light of such incidents, knowledge of Indian culture and language was especially valued. Junior officers like Captain Ebenezer Denny, a student of languages spoken by Delaware and Shawnee tribes, were prized and kept close to headquarters, serving as staff officers to the commanding general.[49]

Perhaps no officer was as important to the diplomatic effort on the frontier as Major John F. Hamtramck, commander of Fort Knox on the Wabash River from 1787 to 1793. A native Canadian who joined the American Army in the Revolution to fight the British, Hamtramck's Catholic faith, fluency in French, and overall care for the civilian populace endeared him to the largely French-descended people of the area. Illustrating such respect, local civilian leaders sent a commendatory letter to the newly arrived American civilian leadership in 1790, noting "the just and humane attention paid by Major Hamtramck during his whole command" which merits the "gratitude and esteem (of) every citizen of Vincennes."[50] Such positive relations between the local people and Hamtramck were likely indispensable to the relatively smooth transition to American rule in the area around 1790. Hamtramck played an important role negotiating with tribes along the Wabash, attempting to prevent the Wea, Potawatomie, and related tribes from joining an anti-United States coalition coalesced around the generally more hostile Miami and Shawnee people. His limited achievement in this was overshadowed by British success, prior to 1794, in fermenting and guiding Indian anger against the growing American settler population.[51]

The breadth of Hamtramck's duties as an officer is especially striking in his involvement in the framing of civil laws, as the only real federal official in the area, for the far west frontier until the arrival of territorial government officials in 1790. Hamtramck reported to Harmar that he had drawn up simple laws and overseen the election of civil officers for the Vincennes region around Fort Knox at the request of the townspeople. Hamtramck rather ruefully noted to his approving superior "my code of laws will make you laugh, but I hope you will consider I am neither a lawyer or a legislator. I have done it for the best."[52]

Lieutenant Clark executed his final mission during his 1795 expedition to the encroaching Spanish fort along the Mississippi, fulfilling Wayne's request for maps and information on the disposition of Spanish posts on the Mississippi, distances, and navigational hazards. Wayne, recognizing the skill behind the valuable reports and maps, forwarded them to Washington.[53] Shortly afterwards, Clark resigned his commission to seek a greater fortune, but in this final mission again executed a task commonly directed to Army officers.

President Washington and Secretary Knox were ever eager for cartographic and navigational information, as well as descriptions of activities of Indian tribes and agents and outposts of the British, Spanish, and French governments along the frontier. Acting on such orders, Harmar sent Ensign Nathan McDowell on an exploration toward Lake Erie, directing the young officer to "ascertain the navigation down the Lake, estimating as accurately as possible, the distances from remarkable places in both waters, noting particularly all obstructions . . . You will continue to transmit me all the Indian news which you can gather."[54] Similarly, Lieutenant John Armstrong was dispatched in 1789 on a secret mission into Spanish-owned land to explore the Mississippi and Missouri Rivers. Ordered to dress like Indians and to disavow any connection with the United States if caught, Armstrong's small party reached only to the mouth of the Missouri River but did provide maps of the Missouri River environs, based on French and Spanish maps discovered in St. Louis.[55] Army officers repeatedly performed such exploring missions, establishing a tradition more famously illustrated by Lewis and Clark's Corps of Discovery and Lieutenant Zebulon Pike's expeditions the following decade.

Clearly, early American officers possessed extensive and broad experience, whether gained through the Revolution or developed through the widely-varied challenges demanded by frontier operations. Experience of course, does not guarantee military expertise. In the final analysis, as *The Army* recognizes, expertise is not judged by knowledge or experience but by competence, or the application of knowledge and experience. In order to characterize the nature of military expertise in the early Army officer corps, it is therefore necessary to evaluate the competence of the officer corps during the three major campaigns during Washington's administration. The following pages examine officer expertise in several of the most critical areas, including an ability to link campaign goals with national strategy, an understanding of the operational environment, operations and training, intelligence, and logistics.

The Washington administration's original strategic plan for the frontier focused on setting conditions for continued white settlement free from Indian raids, while seeking to eliminate critical British support to tribes hostile to the United States. Realizing that both justice and economy indicated this was best done by diplomatic means, with both British and tribal leaders, Washington and Knox initially tried to limit white aggression toward Indian tribes, even using the young Army to destroy illegal white settlements north of the Ohio River.[56] By 1790, it was clear that raids and atrocities by both British-supported Indians and Kentucky settlers, required a response by the administration. Knox therefore called on Harmar, overseen by Northwest Territory Governor St. Clair, to execute a raid focused on punishing tribes guilty of raids along the Ohio River. Knox outlined a very limited and relatively small raid of a suggested force of 400 men, composed of both regulars and militiamen. Failing to understand or appreciate the administration's wider goal of avoiding larger conflict, and urged on by vengeful frontier settlers, St. Clair and Harmar planned an expedition of approximately 1,500 men that in size and scope went well beyond Knox's direction for a limited raid. This larger force and slow rate of advance northwards inspired greater Indian hostility, the exact opposite result intended by the administration. Thus in 1790, both St. Clair and Harmar failed to adequately link campaign goals with the overall strategy, while Washington and Knox failed to ensure that their leaders on the frontier adhered to their overall policy.[57]

The failure of the 1790 offensive focused the administration's attention on the importance of linking campaign ends with the overall strategy. Consequently, Knox's directives to St. Clair were much more direct than those of the previous year. Political fallout over the failure of Harmar's expedition, combined with heightened Indian aggression due to their victory, forced Washington and Knox to abandon their primarily diplomatic focus and urge St. Clair to accomplish a quick and decisive victory over the victorious and growing Indian coalition. Over-reacting to the previous year's failure, the administration failed to give St. Clair, now serving simultaneously as territorial governor and commanding general, with much room to practice operational art, pushing him to initiate operations before the winter of 1791 regardless of his force's readiness. This clearly frustrated St. Clair, yet he failed to adequately understand or articulate to the administration that the greater strategy was placed in far greater jeopardy by his untrained mix of militia and regulars advancing before they were ready, than by a slight delay in initiating the offensive. This operational failure, influenced by both civilian and military leaders, led to the near-destruction of St. Clair's Army in September of 1791, and again resulted in the exact opposite of the strategic intent behind the campaign, leading to an increase in Indian attacks and a strengthening of the hostile tribal confederacy.[58]

After the debacle overseen by St. Clair, both the administration and the new commander, General Wayne, demonstrated a far greater appreciation for the importance of linking campaign goals with national strategy. The much improved relationship between civilian and military leaders in the Fallen Timbers campaign resulted from both civil and military leaders finally realizing the essential need for such political-military synchronization. By 1792, the Washington administration and Wayne recognized the importance of balancing the empowerment of senior Army leaders with ensuring those leaders understood and supported national policy. Correspondence between Wayne and Knox, despite the four- to 10-week turnaround time for communications, was consistently candid; such honest dialogue was of fundamental importance in the skillful synchronization of Wayne's plans and actions with diplomatic overtures in a coordinated pursuit of prioritized objectives.[59]

While frustrated at times by the political-inspired limitations placed upon his Legion, Wayne clearly understood the critical need to ensure Army actions supported the overall strategy. Thus in August 1792, Wayne dismissed a plan by Indian agent Israel Putnam to conduct operations along the Great Lakes, fearing that such an action would cause the heretofore covert British assistance to become open, while undermining ongoing diplomatic and political efforts to cajole England into stopping support to tribes hostile to the United States.[60] Having failed to link campaign and strategic goals prior to 1792, civil and military leaders thus learned to skillfully coordinate plans and goals. Wayne's Fallen Timbers campaign benefited mightily from such synchronization, with British support to hostile tribes minimized by the administration's diplomatic efforts. The expertise shown by Wayne in adapting his campaign to national policy played an especially vital role in the profound consequences of the victory at Fallen Timbers, so evident in the sweeping concessions gained in the subsequent Treaty of Greeneville.[61]

Linked to this appreciation for the strategic situation, Wayne and his officer corps developed a much-improved understanding of the operational environment following the disastrous campaigns of 1790 and 1791. Harmar and St. Clair clearly underestimated the enemy during these offensives, failing to comprehend that the hostile confederation was a dangerous enemy. As described in the introduction of this study, Harmar's foolish division of his Army into multiple columns operating beyond the support of his main force demonstrated a fatal overconfidence, resulting in the loss of over 150 men and a retreat to Fort Washington.[62] To an even greater extent, St. Clair failed to perceive the danger of his position during his campaign of 1791. He clearly perceived the poor training and the overall weakness of his mixed force of regular and militia forces. Multiple subordinate officers demonstrated in their journals a growing unease of the Army's dangerous predicament of being deep in enemy territory, without clear knowledge of the enemy and supported poorly by tenuous lines of support. St. Clair however, continued his offensive, relying on a faulty confidence based on an unfounded dismissal of the willingness of the Indians to confront his relatively large Army.[63] The rout of his Army, described in chapter 1 of this paper, thus resulted in large part from a complete failure to understand his perilous operational environment. In contrast, Wayne declaring that his foe was "an artful enemy," skilled at ambush, surprise and striking at the most favorable moment, built his campaign on a respect for the tribal confederation's dangerous abilities.[64] Wayne's focus on intelligence and security – described later in this chapter - contrast sharply with St. Clair's failure to adequately attend to such matters, and clearly demonstrates St. Clair's mediocrity as a battlefield commander, while showing Wayne's expert understanding of the environment.

Expertise in conducting operations and in a focus on effective training in support of such operations was limited during the early years of the Northwest Indian War. Training failures, so evident in the undisciplined and unreliable troops of the 1790 and 1791 campaigns, were not the exclusive faults of the Army's leadership. Throughout the Northwest Indian War, financial concerns led to the militia and volunteer forces joining regular forces at the very last moment before campaign initiation.

For instance, General Scott's 1,500 Kentuckians fully arrived in camp on 27 July 1794 and the combined Army of regulars and these mounted troops began their offensive on the very next day![65] It is therefore not surprising that one of the most constant trends among regular officers during this period was disappointment over the indiscipline and unreliability of state troops. More fully explored in this study's later chapter on esprit, it is evident that suspicion, discord, animosity, and confusion characterized Army-militia relations during both the 1790 and 1791 offensives. Given this inability to focus on combined training, it was imperative that leaders utilize components of their force in such a way that leveraged strengths while minimizing weaknesses. Both Harmar and St. Clair utterly failed to accomplish this.

During the 1790 campaign, Harmar showed a real lack of expertise in his operational planning and leadership. Clearly realizing that the militia was poorly trained, he failed to leverage the greater discipline and training of his regulars, employing only 20 percent of his more disciplined and trained regulars against the enemy while allowing nearly all of his state forces to engage hostile Indians. His piecemeal deployment of large militia columns supported by small federal detachments far from the main body of regulars allowed Indian ambushes free from the fear of pursuit by the main body. Finally, the continuous splitting of his forces into smaller and smaller columns provided the enemy with superb opportunities to sequentially ambush and defeat each column.[66]

St. Clair's efforts also suffered from a failure to leverage the strengths of his mixed force. Beset by supply problems throughout the campaign, the commander made a critical error shortly before the decisive battle, sending one of his Army's two regular regiments, under the command of Lieutenant Colonel Hamtramck, to protect a supply convoy. This decision resulted in this entire regiment missing the catastrophic battle several days later. While St. Clair refused to blame this decision for the ensuing defeat, sending half of his regular Army strength away on the eve of the battle , while continuing his offensive, seems a clear operational error.[67] St. Clair compounded his predicament by a poor use of his militia forces on the eve of the battle, failing to use them to adequately reconnoiter and positioning them across a creek from the main Army, again denying these less disciplined forces the immediate support of regular troops. Little Turtle's surprise attack early the next morning struck these separated militia, routing them directly into the main camp and throwing the entire Army into a confusion from which it never recovered.[68]

General Wayne's operations benefited from far more preparatory time than was granted to previous commanders. Starting in 1792, Wayne' officer corps focused on training for the coming offensive, two years in the future. Individual, collective, combined arms, and Army-militia training and war games were all stressed. At the heart of all training were officers who were required to attend morning and evening parade and to pay the most "assiduous attention" to the "maneuvering and perfecting (of) the Troops."[69] Again and again, Wayne ordered his officers to lead training, directing that "officers be always with their sub-legions . . . to the end that the Soldiery may be under their eye and acquainted with their voice."[70] The reorganization of the federal Army under Wayne's officer corps into a Legion consisting of four sub-legions, each consisting of two battalions of infantry and a third of riflemen, supported by organic dragoons and tasked artillery units, supported the vision of effective combined arms operations. Wayne articulated this vision, explaining to Knox that all training was directed to operational readiness in which "the riflemen believe in that arm, the Infantry in heavy buck shot and the bayonet, the Dragoons in the sword, & the Legion in their United prowess."[71]

In the field, Wayne and his subordinates demonstrated an improved operational ability. On the march, Wayne skillfully leveraged the strengths of non-regular forces, using them for constant scouting missions and screening operations. Wayne's devotion to the idea gleaned from Caesar's *Commentaries* that the wise commander positioned his force relative to the enemy in a way that all but ensured success was coupled with an understanding from his Revolutionary War experiences about the power of the disciplined use of the bayonet, and the exploitation potential of encircling cavalry. By August 1794, Wayne had positioned his combined forces in such a way that ensured all elements were within supporting distance of one another, while ensuring freedom of maneuver and initiative was enjoyed by his forces and denied to hostile Indians. At Fallen Timbers, the officer corps' ability to synchronize infantry and cavalry maneuvers in the tangled woods of the battlefield clearly indicated the growing expertise of the young Army's officer corps.[72] By 1794, the confidence of Wayne's subordinate officers, especially when compared to the unease of subordinates in the previous campaigns, is striking and reveals Wayne's successful focus on training and operational skill.[73]

Supporting the greater leveraging of both federal and state forces, Wayne' officer corps developed a far greater level of coordination and respect with the Kentucky mounted volunteers than in previous campaigns. As described in greater detail in chapter 6 of this thesis, Wayne rejected the level of militia autonomy maintained in earlier offensives, successfully demanded that Knox establish a distinct chain of command, with Wayne as the clear commander in chief of the mixed force. For the first time, the Department of War established a clear relationship among regular and state officers, with militia officers made subordinate to federal officers of comparative or senior rank, and with regular officers subordinate to militia officers of senior rank.[74] Wayne's measured and integrated use of the Kentucky volunteers and other irregular assets, employed for reconnaissance and scouting missions well within range of the Legion's support, points to a vastly improved appreciation for both the strengths and weaknesses of non-regular elements in the Army.[75]

Expertise in operational skill was closely tied to the able use of intelligence and appropriate security measures to protect the Army against a foe often focused on the use of surprise and ambush. During the 1790 campaign, Harmar and his fellow officers demonstrated an insightful grasp of the importance of intelligence and the protection of the main body from surprise during the approximately 160-mile advance to Kekionga. Travelling cautiously, covering an average of 12 miles a day, Harmar and his officers insisted on the nightly establishment of breastworks and the formation of a square to prevent infiltration or surprise, as well as the daily use of scouts to reconnoiter well ahead of the main body.[76] Harmar's fusing of principles from both Steuben and Bouquet show an ability to take the Army's doctrine and apply it to the environment, an important element of military expertise for any senior officer.[77]

As previously noted, St. Clair's directive ordering one of his two regiments away from the main Army while deep in hostile territory indicates the atrocious nature and use of intelligence during his campaign. Unlike Harmar, who repeatedly stressed the importance of finding and describing the enemy, St. Clair seemed sanguine even while admitting just days before the battle that he thought his "force sufficient, though I have no manner of information as to the force collected to oppose us."[78] Misusing valuable intelligence assets like a friendly band of Chickasaw scouts by sending them on a 10-day mission that took them far from his force, St. Clair seems to have paid little attention to the urgent need to locate his enemy, who in fact were over 1,000 strong, were less than 75 miles away, and were fully apprised of the strength and disposition of St. Clair's Army. St. Clair's aide, Captain Denny, acknowledged this powerful failure, noting in his journal that "one most important object was wanting; can't say neglected, but more might have been done toward obtaining it; this was, a knowledge of the collected force and situation of the enemy; of this (we) were perfectly ignorant."[79]

In addition to the great weaknesses in terms of intelligence expertise, Army leaders in 1791 inexplicably allowed poor levels of security deep in the heart of hostile territory. On the evening of 2 November 1791, after a mix-up regarding the intended camp site for the night, the Army arrived at their designated camp site at dusk. Due to tiredness and lack of discipline, coupled with no perceived eminent threat, little effort was made to ensure that normal standards of security were established. At dawn the next day, Little Turtle's warriors struck with great ferocity and with near total surprise, overwhelming St. Clair's little Army. In the ensuing rout, the worst defeat at the hands of American Indians in United States history, over 650 Soldiers were killed and over 270 wounded.

The understanding and use of intelligence were vastly improved by Wayne and his officer corps after 1792. Wayne's innovative use of scouts led by proven frontiersman Ephraim Kibby and the half-Indian William Wells, the utilization of secret agents seeking information on British involvement and plans, the heavy use of the mounted volunteers from Kentucky to screen the main body, and a focus on counter-intelligence skillfully leveraged skills possessed by elements within the force. Wayne's careful advance, so noted by multiple journals and diaries from subordinate officers, was marked by constant reconnaissance parties sent in all directions and careful daily securing of camps. Revealingly, Wayne's officer corps anticipated to the very day the timing of the decisive battle, ensuring all was in absolute readiness for the decisive battle and that hostile Indians were denied opportunities for ambush and surprise.[80] Thus, Wayne's success in limiting the enemy's initiative is strikingly revealed in the hostile tribes' respectful nick-naming Wayne 'Blacksnake' and 'he who never sleeps.'[81] Thus, the drastic improvement in the use of intelligence and careful security precautions under General Wayne is impressive and reveals the development of a high level of expertise by Wayne and his officers that led to the decisive victory at Fallen Timbers.

Unlike the vast improvements developed in the officer corps in terms of operational art, training and battlefield leadership, intelligence and security, logistical expertise bedeviled Army leaders from 1789 to 1796. In all three campaigns, difficulties in adequately supplying a large and mobile force significantly impacted operations. During Harmar's campaign, one of the two arms of the planned pincer movement failed due to supply problems. This arm under Hamtramck, intended to draw pressure from Harmar's main effort, came to an abrupt halt only two weeks into the campaign, when Army contractors failed to provide adequate rations, and the militia attached to his command refused to continue without full rations.

The supporting column therefore returned to Fort Knox, having failed to accomplish their primary purpose because of a failure of logistics.[82]

Similarly, during St. Clair's offensive in 1791, supply difficulties negatively influenced operations. As noted earlier, shortages led to desertions and forced the Army to wait for supply convoys to catch up to the main body; St. Clair felt forced to dispatch a regiment to protect supplies on the eve of battle, when these regulars were desperately needed.[83] Supply difficulties increased as the Army proceeded farther from the base of supply at Fort Washington. According to Denny's journal entry for late October 1791, logistical failures made it impracticable to continue operations, noting in his journal: "forage entirely destroyed; horses failing and cannot be kept up; provisions from hand to mouth."[84]

Logistical failures continued to plague the Army after St. Clair's defeat. Multiple journals from Wayne's officers of all ranks decry the consistent failure of the contractors to supply flour, meat, and forage for the horses and cattle accompanying the Army.[85] The extension of the campaign into 1794 resulted in large part from Wayne's refusal to advance deep into hostile territory until some of the critical shortages were supplied. Wayne attempted to resolve some of the earlier issues, establishing a quartermaster department led by Lieutenant Colonel James O'Hara and Major Isaac Craig but deeper institutional weaknesses continued to strain logistical problems.[86] The final decisive victory in 1794 occurred in spite of the amateurish nature of logistics support to the Army. Throughout this period, the lack of logistical specialists within the officer corps left the entire Army at the mercy of contractors largely unwilling or unable to adhere to their contracts. The Army's total lack of any organic support infrastructure resulted in a total reliance on contract supply and again and again, the contractors failed to meet their requirements. This reality consistently and severely limited the officer corps' flexibility and freedom of maneuver during operations.

In summary, it is clear that despite the lack of any formal system of military education available to the officer corps of the early Army, alternative means were utilized to gain valued military knowledge. Such self-development was likely spotty with some officers probably eschewing self-development through study. Yet the belief and example of senior leaders like Washington, Knox, Harmar, St. Clair, and Wayne ensured that military knowledge was pursued by a significant number of Army officers. Perhaps even more importantly, the broad and demanding experiences challenging the officer corps between 1789 and 1796 led to significant levels of the broad knowledge described in today's ADP 1, *The Army*.

These experiences, ranging from battlefield combat to Indian diplomacy to liaising with civil government agencies to exploration expeditions, clearly produced a significant number of officers skilled at applying their knowledge to actual situations. Amateurish levels of leadership and institutional weaknesses, particularly in terms of logistical operations, continued throughout the period; however after 1792, operations were commonly characterized by the skillful application of military knowledge and understanding. In other words, judged by the standards described by the current doctrine on professionalism, many officers developed a substantial level of military expertise by 1796.

Notes

1. Headquarters, Department of the Army, ADP 1, para. 2-10.

2. Headquarters, Department of the Army, ADP 1, para. 2-9; and Headquarters, Department of the Army, *Whitepaper - Our Army Profession,* 6.

3. Headquarters, Department of the Army, ADP 1, para. 2-11.

4. Booraem, 41-44. In the case of young men like Harrison, powerful family connections provided for an exception to Washington's normal policy of restricting commissions to those at least 21 years old because "the lives of men are of too much importance to be confided to a raw youth." Knopf, *Anthony Wayne*, Knox to Wayne, 28 September 1792, 110.

5. Harrison quoted from his correspondence in Gunderson, 3.

6. For Harrison's experience see Booraem and Gunderson. That such an experience was representative is evident in multiple other journals by new officers like William Clark, William Eaton, Thomas Underhill, and Hugh Brady.

7. Mark Puls, *Henry Knox: Visionary General of the American Revolution.* (New York, NY: Palgrave Macmillan, 2008), 136.

8. George Washington, "Washington's Eighth Annual Message to Congress, 7 December 1796," *The George Washington Papers,* Alderman Library, University of Virginia, Charlottesville, VA, 26 September 1796, http://gwpapers.virginia.edu (accessed 7 May 2013).

9. Senator Ralph Izard quoted Washington in a 2 January 1795 letter to his wife in John C. Fredriksen, "A Tempered Sword Untested: the Military Career of General George Izard (Part I)," *The Journal of America's Military Past* 25, no. 2 (Fall, 1998): 7.

10. Izard.

11. Arthur P. Wade, "Artillerists and Engineers: The Beginnings of American Seacoast Fortifications, 1794-1815" (Ph.D. diss., Kansas State University, Manhattan, KS, 1977), 39-69 is valuable for its discussion of the obscure attempts by the Washington administration to establish an academy at West Point in the mid-1790s.

12. John Fredriksen, *The United States Army in the War of 1812: Concise Biographies of Commanders and Operational Histories of Regiments with Bibliographies of Published and Primary Resources* (Jefferson, NC: McFarland and Company), 79.

13. Asa Bird Gairdner, "Henry Burbeck: Brevet Brigadier-General United States Army—Founder of the United States Military Academy," *The Magazine of American History* 9 (January, 1883): 258.

14. Gairdner, 262. Fredriksen's brief biography of Burbeck in *The United States Army in the War of 1812: Concise Biographies,* 79, is more measured about such a title for Burbeck but accepts that he is entitled to "some credit" for the creation of the academy at West Point.

15. See Huntington, 19-20, 237-241; and Allan R. Millett, *Military Professionalism and Officership in America* (Columbus, OH: Mershon Center of the Ohio State University, 1977), 2-3.

16. Huntington, *The Soldier and the State*, convincingly describes these vocational patterns of the eighteenth century, though he draws the unfortunate conclusion that such patterns necessarily precluded the development of military professionalism.

17. Friedrich Wilhelm Ludolf Gerhard Augustin Steuben, *Baron Von Steuben's Revolutionary War Drill Manual.* 1794. Reprint, New York, NY: Dover Publications, 1985.

18. Steuben, 103, 134.

19. Walter Kretchik, *US Army Doctrine: From the American Revolution to the War on Terror* (Lawrence, KS: University Press of Kansas, 2011), 25-33.

20. Guthman, 9-20.

21. Knopf, *Anthony Wayne*, Wayne to Knox, 13 September 1792, 94.

22. Knopf, *Orderly Books of the United States Legion* reveal this consistent focus on standardizing order and discipline in Wayne's Legion in accordance with Steuben, *Baron Von Steuben's Revolutionary War Drill Manual. Regulations*.

23. John B. Linn, ed., "Reminiscences of Hugh Brady," in *Annals of Buffalo Valley, Pennsylvania, 1755-1855* (Harrisburg, PA: L. S. Hart, printer, 1877), 178.

24. Booraem, 86, 108.

25. Jones, 126.

26. Higginbotham, *George Washington and the American Military Tradition,* 14-18, 78.

27. Puls, 14-21; and Sandra Powers, "Studying the Art of War: Military Books Known to American Officers and Their French Counterparts during the Second Half of the Eighteenth Century," *The Journal of Military History* 70 (July, 2006): 781-814, persuasively argues for Knox's extensive knowledge of martial works, including familiarity with thinkers like Saxe, Vauban, Blondel, and Muller.

28. John Mahon, "Pennsylvania and the Beginnings of the Regular Army," *Pennsylvania History* 21 (January 1954): 42.

29. John Steinle, "Unlucky Soldier: Josiah Harmar's Frontier Struggle," *Timeline* 8 (April/May 1991): 9.

30. Frazer E. Wilson, *Arthur St. Clair: Rugged Ruler of the Northwest* (Richmond, VA: Garrett and Massie, 1944), 21.

31. Nelson, *Anthony Wayne*, 15.

32. Nelson, Wayne to Washington, 2 September 1777, 50.

33. Indications of attention to self-development through reading is evident in William Henry Harrison's appreciation for military history in his correspondence as a junior officer (Booraem, 108) and in Colonel John F. Hamtramck's small library of military tactics as related by F. Clever Bald, "Colonel John Francis Hamtramck," *Indiana Magazine of History* 44 (December, 1948) 353.

34. Washington revealed his reasons for St. Clair's selection in a letter to St. Clair reprinted in Smith, *The St. Clair Papers*, 283; the rationale behind the selection of Wayne in 1792 is ably described in Kohn, *Eagle and Sword,* 125-126.

35. Harmar's biographical information is drawn primarily from Steinle, 2-17.

36. St. Clair's biographical information is drawn primarily from Wilson, *Arthur St. Clair*.

37. Wayne's biographical information is drawn primarily from Nelson, *Anthony Wayne*.

38. Figures are drawn from biographical entries in Heitman.

39. Knopf, *Anthony Wayne*, Wayne to Knox, 21 September 1792, 107.

40. Jones, 62-67.

41. The papers and journals of officers like Ensign Jacob Melcher, Lieutenants William Henry Harrison, John Armstrong, and William Peters, and Captains Jonathon Heart and William Ferguson reveal how common such duty was for young officers.

42. Jones, 68.

43. St. Clair, 152-154.

44. Smith, *The St. Clair Papers*, Harmar to Knox, 14 January 1790, 129.

45. Jones, 71.

46. Knopf, *Anthony Wayne*, Wayne to Knox, 17 September 1793, 272.

47. Jones, 86-89.

48. Sword, 212.

49. Ebenezer Denny studied these languages during his service in the Confederation Army in the 1780s, compiling a nearly 800 word vocabulary which was included in the publication Ebenezer Denny, *Military Journal of Major Ebenezer Denny* (Philadelphia, PA: J. B. Lippincott & Co., 1860), 274-281.

50. Thornbrough, *Outpost on the Wabash Letters,* 19, 241.

51. During his six-year command at Fort Knox, Hamtramck was constantly engaged in trying to negotiate alliances with various Indian tribes, based on guidance received from both civilian and military superiors. For example, see letters between Governor of the Northwest Territory St. Clair, General Harmar and Hamtramck in 1790 in Thornbrough, *Outpost on the Wabash Letters*, 222-247.

52. Thornbrough, Hamtramck to Harmar, 13 April 1788, 71.

53. Jones, 92.

54. Guthman, Harmar to McDowell, 4 February 1790, 83.

55. Colton Storm, "Lieutenant Armstrong's Expedition to the Missouri River," *Mid-America: An Historical Review* 14, no. 3 (1943): 181.

56. In the late 1780s, Harmar sent out detachments to destroy illegal white settlements north of the Ohio River, as described by Jacobs, 22-23. This supported the original desire by Washington and Knox for a peaceful resolution to the crisis between whites and Indians, ending in the gradual absorption of peaceful Indians into white society. The constant pressure from white settlers for more land claimed by tribes and the vicious cycle of brutal raids from both sides doomed their vision. Both sides consistently violated the Ohio River divide, agreed upon earlier, leading to ever-greater tensions along the northwest frontier. The administration's hope of "humanity and absorption" is evident in Washington's and Knox's correspondence and is well described in Ward, *The Department of the Army*, 142.

57. The best source for a discussion of the coordination between the Washington administration and the Army's leaders is Kohn, *Eagle and Sword*, 100-108.

58. Kohn, *Eagle and Sword*, 100-108, convincingly describes St. Clair's failures to adequately understand his operating environment, as does his correspondence in the post-defeat publication of St. Clair.

59. The impressive level of candor, respect, and trust between Knox and Wayne is evident throughout their correspondence, reprinted in Knopf, *Anthony Wayne*.

60. Knopf, *Anthony Wayne*, Wayne to Knox, 24 August 1792, 73.

61. In addition to the impressive coordination evident in the letters between Knox and Wayne found throughout Knopf, Anthony Wayne; both Sword, and Kohn, *Eagle and Sword* ably describe the dense political and military coordination that occurred during Wayne's campaign, as well as the failed synchronization during earlier efforts.

62. Michael Warner, "General Josiah Harmar's Campaign Reconsidered: How the Americans Lost the Battle of Kekionga," *Indiana Magazine of History* 83, no. 1 (March 1987): 47-55.

63. Sword, St. Clair to Knox, 4 September 1791, 168.

64. Knopf, *Anthony Wayne*, Wayne to Knox, 27 April 1793, 229-230.

65. Knopf, *Anthony Wayne*, Wayne to Knox, 27 July 1794, 349-350. Financial concerns were based on the federal government funding the cost of mobilizing and utilizing the militia and volunteer troops during the campaigns.

66. Warner, 47-64.

67. St. Clair penned *A Narrative of the Manner in Which the Campaign Against the Indians* following his defeat, including his reasoning behind his operational plan and execution of the campaign.

68. Descriptions of St. Clair's battlefield leadership are drawn from James Currie, "The First Congressional Investigation: St. Clair's Military Disaster of 1791," *Parameters* 20 (December 1990): 95-102 and Sword.

69. Knopf, *Orderly Books of the United States Legion,* 16 August 1792, 12.

70. Knopf, July 1793, 49.

71. Knopf, *Anthony Wayne*, Wayne to Knox, 9 May 1893, 235.

72. For Wayne's battlefield expertise during the Fallen Timbers campaign, see Allen Millett, "Caesar and the Northwest: The Wayne Campaign 1792-1795," *Timeline* 14, no. 3 (May/June 1997): 2-21.

73. The unease of officers in previous campaigns is revealed in the journals of Lieutenant Ebenezer Denny, Major Jonathon Heart, and Colonel Winthrop Sargent, while the confidence felt by officers on the eve of Fallen Timbers is evident in the journals of officers like Lieutenants Boyer and William Clark and Major John Buell.

74. Knopf, *Anthony Wayne*, 20 June 1793 and Knox to Wayne, 16 May 1794, 244-245, 327-329.

75. Paul D. Nelson, "General Charles Scott, The Kentucky Mounted Volunteers, and the Northwest Indian Wars, 1784-1794," *Journal of the Early Republic* 6, no. 3 (Fall, 1986): 219-251.

76. Denny, 141-144.

77. For this fusion, see Allan Brown, "The Role of the Army in Western Settlement: Josiah Harmar's Command, 1785-1790," *Pennsylvania Magazine of History and Biography* 93 (April 1969): 161-178.

78. St. Clair, *A Narrative of the Manner in Which the Campaign Against the Indians*, 224.

79. Denny, 171.

80. Lieutenant William Clark's journal is representative of the confidence and readiness of Wayne's Army as it accurately prepared to meet the enemy the day before the battle. See William Clark, "William Clark's Journal of General Wayne's Campaign," ed. R. C. McGrane, *Mississippi Valley Historical Review* 1 (December 1914): 428.

81. The leader of the hostile Indian confederation facing Wayne, the Shawnee chief Blue Jacket, referred to Wayne in these names based on his careful watchfulness and constant preparedness for Indian attacks. See John G. Heckewelder, *History, Manners and Customs of the Indian Nations who Once Inhabited Pennsylvania and the Neighboring States* (New York, NY: Arno Press, 1971), 192.

82. The supply difficulties during the 1790 campaign are demonstrated throughout Josiah Harmar, *The Proceedings of a Court of Inquiry, held at the special request of Brigadier General Josiah Harmar, Commanding Officer of the Expedition against the Miami Indians, 1790* (Philadelphia, PA: Jehn Fenno, 1791) as well as in the journals of officers like Captain Samuel Newman and Lieutenant Ebenezer Denny.

83. Smith, *The St. Clair Papers,* Clair to Knox, 1 November 1791, 251.

84. Denny, 160.

85. See, for example, Lieutenant Thomas Underwood's repetitive entries in his journal about half-rations in Thomas T. Underwood, *Journal of Thomas Taylor Underwood, March 26, 1792 to March 18, 1800: An Old Soldier in Wayne's Army* (Cincinnati, OH: Society of Colonial Wars in the State of Ohio, 1945).

86. The depth of Wayne's realization of the importance of logistics in the aftermath of the campaign is revealed in his nomination of Captain Henry DeButts to succeed the retiring O'Hara in 1795, noting to Knox that "as the Quarter Master General of this Army is an Officer of the first consequence and Confidence," the best officer to take the position is DeButts, naming him "the most competent Officer belonging to this Army." Knopf, *Anthony Wayne*, Wayne to Knox, 19 September 1795, 460.

Chapter 5
Military Professionalism and Honorable Service in the Early American Army Officer Corps, 1789 - 1796

Following descriptions of trust and military expertise, *The Army* turns to a discussion of the concept of honorable service. Adhering closely to the ideal expressed by the current Army value of selfless service, the manual explains that military professionals commit by public oath to the idea of "unlimited liability." This idea calls for a readiness to sacrifice personal interests in order to support and defend the Constitution while accomplishing assigned missions. Inherent to honorable and selfless service is a willingness to accept the "risk of serious personal harm or death." Service by military professionals is honorable both because it pursues the worthy goal of protecting the United States and its interests, and because such professionals perform their duty in an ethical manner with integrity and respect for Army and American values.[1]

The Army's new doctrine on professionalism closely relates authentic honorable service to the concept of commitment, defined as "being primarily motivated by the intrinsic factors of sacrifice and service to others and to the Nation, rather than being motivated by the extrinsic factors related to a job."[2]

This chapter describes the way officers in the early American Army understood the concept of selfless and honorable service and how they carried out its demands. A variety of tremendous hardships challenged Army officers during this period, demanding considerable sacrifice. This chapter describes those challenges and officers' responses to them, including the development by the officer corps of major patterns of service. It also depicts the way the officer corps grappled with understanding and developing the relationship of their patriotic sacrifice to their own self-interest as well as to American society. A later chapter on stewardship, examines the relationship between military service, professionalism, and ethics.

During the earliest years of the United States Army, officers understood the concept of sacrifice in an immediate and powerful way. Overwhelmingly stationed on the frontier during this period, officers and their Soldiers faced relatively austere living conditions coupled with near-constant danger from hostile Indians. Available garrison orderly books and journals maintained by officers during this time period describe the common recurrence of supply problems, especially food shortage during winter months. Responding to a complaint from Major Hamtramck regarding food shortages at Fort Knox in January 1790, Brigadier General Harmar helplessly noted, "I am truly sorry to hear of the great scarcity of provisions with you, but all the posts are equally distressed in that respect. We have been on the point of starvation here ever since my arrival."[3] Shortages of uniforms, tools, medicine, whiskey and such common necessities as needles and paper frequently populate primary sources and indicate the relative difficulty of life in frontier garrisons.[4] Pay was often in arrears, sometimes by over a year. Difficulties in obtaining funding for pay from Congress and problems in safely transporting cash to the frontier in a timely manner frequent Knox's correspondence with his Army leaders.[5] The nation's fragile economic condition forced Washington and Knox to admonish Army leaders to be frugal. Knox's reminder to Major Henry Gaither in 1793 to manage all operations "with a truly republican economy" was emblematic of frequent warnings and led, at least in part, to the austere living conditions experienced by the Army.[6]

Coupled with such living conditions, the presence of wide-ranging and dangerous Indian tribes demanded courage and a readiness to sacrifice personal comfort and safety. Danger threatened even the most mundane duties. While on a hunting trip in early 1792, Captain Joseph Shaylor – commander of Fort Jefferson – and his small group suffered at the hands of a Shawnee ambush, resulting in the death of Shaylor's son and a painful wound for Shaylor.[7] On a mission bringing supplies to Cherokee tribes along the Tennessee River in March of 1790, Indians attacked Major John Doughty's small detachment of 15 men, resulting in the loss of six killed and five wounded.[8] In the summer of 1790, Ensign Jacob Melcher reported, "the waters are fairly alive with savages;" his experience leading supply expeditions on the Ohio River supported such a claim. Indians attacked his small one-boat detachment in July 1790, killing one and wounding two Soldiers. Less than a year later in the same area, a hostile war-party again struck Melcher's small unit resulting in several Soldiers killed. Melcher, reported Hamtramck, "had the good fortune to escape but lost everything."[9] Such representative experiences indicate the danger that faced officers whenever they left the relative safety of their fortifications.

These dangers and sacrifices paled in comparison to those experienced during combat operations. Enlisted Soldiers in the young Army were generally inexperienced with relatively few veteran non-commissioned officers and they relied especially on the leadership and example of officers during combat. In operations large and small during the Northwest Indian War, officers of all ranks almost always led from the very front. Fighting in the woods and small clearings along the frontier demanded physical courage in facing a fearsome enemy, often in hand-to-hand combat or at extremely close range.[10]

The officer corps generally met this challenge with tremendous bravery. Captain Thomas Underwood's journal recounts the representative bravery of Captain Asa Hartshorne during a 1794 attack on Fort Recovery. When a surprise attack by Miami warriors against a convoy resupplying the fort threatened the caravan escorts, Hartshorne rode out of the fort at the head of a small relief party. Hartshorne's detachment relieved their comrades, driving the Indians into the woods. In the aftermath of this charge however, Indians surrounded and wounded him badly. Ordering his detachment to leave him and escape to the relative safety of the fort's walls, Hartshorne died, sacrificing himself for the survival of his comrades.[11] Major Alexander Trueman accepted his mission as an emissary to the volatile and dangerously unpredictable Miami tribes in early 1792 with great "patriotism and cheerfulness" according to Knox.[12] His death at the hands of the Indians indicates the dangerous nature of officers' service in the old Northwest Territory.

During Harmar's 1790 campaign, regular Army officers engaged against the enemy distinguished themselves by their bravery. Captain John Armstrong's detachment of 30 regulars accompanied several hundred militiamen on a raid. When surprised by an Indian war-party, Armstrong's battlefield leadership kept his men on the field after the rapid retreat of most of the militiamen, slowing the Indian attack but leading to the death of 23 of his detachment. A few days later, the personal bravery of Major John Wyllys steadied his men in fighting off an ambush, though it resulted in his death with almost all of his 60 men.[13]

Great courage by officers characterized St. Clair's 1791 campaign as well. During the decisive battle along the Wabash River, survivors recounted the impressive bravery of leaders. General Richard Butler refused to leave the field after his first wound and when struck down a second time, declined to retreat, ordering others to leave him to his near certain death and to save themselves in the Army's rushed retreat to the south.[14] Acting Adjutant General Winthrop Sargent (not given to undeserved praise), described with few exceptions the overwhelming bravery of the 95 regular officers involved in the battle, illustrating his depiction with the example of Captain John Crawford. Early in the battle, Crawford "received a brace of balls in his body, but that notwithstanding he continued with cheerfulness and spirit to discharge his duty during the service, on foot, in bad roads, without a murmur or complaint, and scarcely ever betraying the symptoms of fatigue or that he was wounded."[15]

Statistics reveal the battlefield presence and sacrifice of officers. At the disaster along the Wabash River in 1791, the regular Army officer corps suffered a 58 percent casualty (killed and wounded) rate, considerably higher than that of militia officers and just slightly higher than the rates experienced by enlisted Soldiers.[16] Such figures support the claim by soldier-participants like Sergeant Jackson Johonnot, writing in the aftermath of the battle, "our officers, rendered conspicuous by their exertions to stimulate the men, became victims of savage ingenuity."[17]

Very few instances of a lack of such bravery seem to exist. Critics strikingly charged Harmar with cowardice and drunkenness following his disappointing campaign of 1790, pointing to his failure to lead from the front during any of the several engagements during the campaign. The Army's subsequent court of inquiry called to investigate the campaign's failure found no evidence of such faults in the commanding general, but the leveling of such accusations indicates the existence of significant expectations regarding officer courage.[18] Assessed as a whole, the actions of the officer corps during this early period reveal the development of a strong tradition of officer bravery and selfless service in the field.

The living conditions, financial foundation of the Army, danger, and casualties suffered by the officer corps seriously influenced the nature of officers' service to the republic, leading to a significant level of instability. In early 1793, General Wayne complained to the Secretary of War that Congressional attempts to reduce the size of the Army and reduce the pay of both officers and men resulted in "a very visible and injurious effect upon the minds of the Officers, many of whom have already resigned and others are determined to follow their example . . . in fact those who wish to continue in the service conceive that they hold their Commissions, on a very precarious tenor."[19] Historian William Skelton's scholarship rightly emphasizes instability within the officer corps, noting for example, that 61 percent of officers in the service in 1789 no longer held commissions in 1795. Skelton's argument that "for the thirty years following the Revolution, the most important characteristic of the Army officer corps was the instability of its membership" is overstated, as this thesis seeks to show, but instability within the officer corps was a constant reality.[20] Representative examples from the early officer corps clearly reveal this volatility.

Ebenezer Denny seemed intent upon a military career from a young age. As a teenager, he served on an American privateer preying on British merchant ships until gaining a commission as a 19-year-old ensign in the Continental Army in 1780. Following the war, Denny remained in the service as General Harmar's aide and acting adjutant in the 1790 campaign and earning praise from Governor St. Clair that the young officer "had every quality that I could wish a young man to possess, who meant to make the army a profession."[21] By 1791, Denny evidently had changed his mind about his profession, noting in the aftermath of the St. Clair-led debacle and after nearly seven years spent in frontier warfare that "I feel perfectly weary and sick of the noise and bustle of a military life."[22]

The example of Captain Erskurius Beatty reveals the corrosive results of a lack of a sound financial footing for the Army. A six-year Revolutionary War veteran, Beatty's commitment to the military profession led to his rejoining the Army as a lieutenant and the service's paymaster in 1784. In this role, his difficulties in acquiring necessary funds to support the Army resulted in tremendous frustration and seem eventually to have led to his resignation in 1792. Beatty declared after a particularly unsuccessful trip to Philadelphia to gather funds from the government, that the Army's shaky financial situation "makes me wish the devil had them all, and sincerely curse the day that ever induced me again to enter in such a rascally service, when cringing sycophants in the midst of plenty, kick the poor worn out soldier out of the door."[23]

Similarly, Lieutenant William Henry Harrison, after early declarations of contentment with a military career, grew frustrated with the instability that characterized the early Army. Commissioned in 1792, Harrison focused diligently on becoming a military professional and his hard work and dedication bore fruit; his service and his family connections led to a place on Wayne's staff during the Fallen Timbers campaign, followed by selection to command the Army's premier frontier post at Fort Washington. Promotion seemed close with Wayne recommending Harrison as "a Young Gentleman of family, Education, and merit."[24] In 1796, in the aftermath of the victory over hostile Indians in the Northwest Indian War, Congress re-organized the Army, only slightly reducing the total number of officers but more substantially limiting prospects for increased pay and promotions within the officer corps. Like many others, this legislative reaction to the victory gained by the Army angered Lieutenant Harrison and he declared, "the very illiberal treatment with which I have met from the government has determined me to abandon the profession of arms entirely in a short time."[25] Harrison remained in the service until he was able to find a suitable next career, resigning in early 1798 after six years of service.

Other causes of instability, examined in the following two chapters, included friction and animosity within the officer corps and a drive by senior leaders to purge the corps of unprofessional officers. These factors, combined with the common occurrence of officer deaths in battle, the constant danger and poor living conditions on the frontier, and a lack of consistent governmental support related to prospects for pay and promotion, seriously undermined the commitment of many officers for long-term service.

A significant number of officers, however, successfully navigated these impediments and served as officers for a full career, with some fighting in three major wars. For instance, Henry Burbeck served as an officer for 37, from 1775 to 1815, with only a three-year hiatus in the 1780s, rising to the rank of brevet brigadier general. From his service as an ensign in 1777, until his death while serving as a brevet brigadier general in 1822, Moses Porter's career as an officer spanned 45 years with only a brief break under the Confederation government. Jacob Kingsbury started his service as a private in 1775, earning a commission in 1780. He later served as an officer from 1787 to 1815, ending his career as a colonel after 36 years of military service. Commissioned in 1792, Daniel Bissell served continuously for 30 years until 1821, rising to the rank of brevet brigadier general.[26] Such examples are unusual but not especially rare. Of the approximately 190 Army officers identified as serving between 1789 and 1795, at least 19 served over 20 years as regular Army officers with a significantly larger number serving over 10 years.[27] These examples of long service indicate the emerging development, despite serious obstacles, of the presence of career officers within the Army and a resulting island of stability among the volatility of service life.

All officers, regardless of the length of their service, confronted strong obstacles to professional service. In their response to such impediments, the officer corps began to develop significant patterns in the nature of their military service. One such feature was a belief that professional and patriotic service did not preclude an element of self-interest. This was not a new realization. After the decline of popular support for service in the Continental Army in the Revolution, General Washington ruefully concluded, "few men are capable of making a continual sacrifice of . . . private interest or advantage, to the common good."[28] Thus, Washington urged Congress to provide officers with half-pay after the Revolution, in order to encourage leaders to serve. During the 1790s, officers focused on receiving the recognition, respect and gratitude that they felt their honorable service deserved. On the eve of Wayne's 1794 offensive, newly promoted and 17-year veteran Lieutenant Colonel Hamtramck insisted to General Harmar "if I had not been promoted I should have resigned this spring."[29] While the Army's adherence to a system of promotion by seniority generally limited disagreements within the regular officer corps, officers resented any perceived encroachments on their honor, reputation, or standing as military gentlemen. In 1794, Lieutenant Harrison responded to familial doubts about his long-term prospects in the Army, proudly noting to his brother "while I wear an officer's sword and the livery of my country I will not disgrace them by owning myself inferior to any person."[30]

The career of Major Thomas Butler perhaps best exemplifies this tendency to fuse a concern for an officer's individual honor and rights with a devotion to honorable service to the republic. Brother to General Richard Butler and two other officer-brothers and a highly regarded seven-year Revolutionary War veteran, Major Butler rejoined the Army in 1791 for St. Clair's campaign. Badly wounded in the Army's defeat along the Wabash, he served throughout the 1790s, earning promotion to lieutenant colonel in 1795 and then to colonel in 1799. A long running dispute with the ranking Army officer, Brigadier General James Wilkinson, escalated in 1801 when Butler refused to cut his hair queue in accordance with Wilkinson's Army-wide order. Calling the order "impertinent, arbitrary, and illegal," Butler insisted his superior officer had no right to dictate an order intruding upon his personal rights, writing to his friend Andrew Jackson that he intended to "adhere to my old principles, the laws of my country."[31] Wilkinson responded by suspending Butler from command and ordering a court martial, though Butler died of natural causes before it concluded butler's final act was to order a hole to be cut into his coffin, allowing his illegal queue to hang out of it, so that "the damned old rascal (Wilkinson) will see that, even when dead, I refuse to obey his order."[32] Obviously, a somewhat bizarre case, it is revealing. It illustrates, in an admittedly extreme manner, the way the young officer corps struggled to maintain a sense of personal honor and respect for the individual officer with the demands of long-term service devoted to sacrificial service for a greater good.[33]

The officer corps' insistence on respect, both for the individual officer and the officer corps as a whole, led to regular officers often rejecting the idea of serving under militia officers. Captain John Armstrong felt a sense of "humiliation" when directed to serve under a senior militia officer in late 1788; in the aftermath of Harmar's campaign, Armstrong vowed never to fight with or be commanded by militia officers.[34] Harmar approved of his subordinate's perspective, noting in 1789 "no person can hold a more contemptible opinion of the militia than I do."[35] This common view and the struggle to develop a working relationship between regular, militia, and volunteer forces persisted throughout this period. The following chapter, on esprit within the officer corps, examines this in more detail, but the representative attitude of officers like Armstrong indicates both a sense of pride in the regular service of the officer corps and the need to grapple with tense relations among regular and non-regular officers.

Officers were not the only Soldiers experiencing a sense of volatility in the Army; enlisted men likely suffered even more due to organizational instability. The officer corps' reaction to this reality reveals a struggle to develop a paternal sense of care for enlisted Soldiers. As in so many other instances, Revolutionary War tradition proved important as a precedent. Washington's vision for officer-enlisted relations insisted on a relationship balanced between Soldiers' need to respect discipline and hierarchical authority and the necessity for officers to understand they were leading free citizen-Soldiers. This vision, which Washington strove to inculcate in his Revolutionary officer corps, deeply informed Steuben's *Regulations* and many senior officers who continued their Revolutionary War service into the 1790s. Washington's famous and superb example of selfless service in the Revolution and his vision outlined in the Army's *Regulations* therefore provided a blueprint and an ideal for the Army's young officer corps' understanding of service-oriented leaders.[36]

Emphasizing to officers that a leader's first object was "to gain the love of his men, by treating them with every possible kindness and humanity," the early Army's doctrinal manual also insisted that commanders "must preserve the strictest discipline and order."[37] This dual charge, generally accepted by officers of the new republic, reflected an understanding of leadership focused on paternal-like service. Further reflecting an important tradition carried over from the Revolution to the 1790s Army, the *Regulations* insisted that an officer always accompany his unit during operations and that "there is no fatigue the Soldiers go through that the officers should not share; and on all occasions they should set them examples of patience and perseverance."[38]

With very few officers devoted to staff-work and with nearly all officers deployed on the frontier, leading from the front and sharing hardships with enlisted Soldiers was somewhat natural. Senior officers like Wayne sought to ensure such conduct by continually reminding officers of his expectation that they would train, inspect, and accompany their Soldiers at all times.[39] Wayne commended selfless service, such as the "example and unremitting industry of the Officers, who nobly and generously submitted to every inconvenience and inclemency of weather living (or rather existing in cold linen tents) until their men are rendered comfortable."[40] Wayne's daily orders to officers reminded them to visit their sick Soldiers, insisting, "the health and Compact of the Soldiers are objects of the first consideration in which both duty and humanity unite."[41] Illustrative of both an attitude of selfless service and continued failures within the logistical system, officers stationed at Fort Defiance in 1795 combined their personal money to purchase hospital stores and liquor for wounded and sick Soldiers. General Harmar, Major Doughty, and Major Hamtramck also reportedly used their personal funds to buy badly needed supplies for Soldiers.[42]

The officer corps' struggle to serve their Soldiers ought not to be mistaken for any sense of professional equality, for most officers perceived their service in a distinctly different manner than the service of enlisted Soldiers. Unlike today's doctrine which implies Soldiers of all ranks can and ought to be professionals, the early officer corps reserved such status to officer ranks. The divide between enlisted and officer was wide and officers generally strove to maintain that separation. Officers typically earned between seven and 20 times the pay of a private.[43] An examination of various orderly books reveals distinctly different standards of discipline afforded enlisted Soldiers and commissioned officers; while ferocious corporal punishment was common for enlisted infractions like desertion and drunkenness, officer crimes like drunkenness and conduct unbecoming an officer usually resulted only in reprimands, suspension, and in rare instances, dismissal from the officer corps.[44] The case of Private Henry Hamilton reveals both this divide and the emerging sense of paternal care for Soldiers. In June of 1792, Hamilton was arrested and court martialed for armed resistance to the orders of Ensign William Divan, evidently threatening the young officer with his bayonet. The court recommended and Wayne approved Hamilton's death sentence to impress upon Soldiers that "a crime of so deep a die, a Soldier who lifts his arm against his Officer ought not to be permitted to live." At the last moment however, upon the intervention of Divan, Hamilton's life was spared."[45]

This perception of distinction from both enlisted Soldiers and militiamen, combined with a partial sense of isolation stemming from the officer corps' frustration with a perceived lack of societal appreciation for the Army's sufferings, marks another significant element in the early officer corps' perception of service. The drawing of such distinctions demonstrates an emerging sense of being different and somehow set apart. While not explicitly a feature of professional military service as described in today's doctrine on professionalism, such a setting apart has commonly been an important component of a definition of military professionalism.[46]

In the 1790s officer corps, this distinction was not definite; a strong tension remained between this sense of separateness and a need to preserve societal trust by remaining true to the concept of the citizen-soldier. A tendency among officers to see themselves as societal leaders first and commissioned officers second, limited a sense of isolation from American society; one of the striking aspects of officer service during this period is how frequently officers practiced service and leadership in roles outside the Army. At times, this pattern took the form of repeated service in the Army, separated by leadership positions outside the Army. Whatever the specific details, early Army officers very frequently devoted themselves to long careers of public service, both in and out of uniform. Lieutenant William Henry Harrison is probably the most famous such example, serving over 40 years as a junior officer, Northwest Territory Secretary and Governor, general officer in the War of 1812, member of Congress, and ambassador to Columbia, before his service as US President. Major General Hugh Brady surpassed even Harrison in time public office, serving as a lieutenant during the Fallen Timbers campaign, an officer in the Virginia Militia, followed by a remarkable 39 straight years as an Army officer, from 1812 to 1851. Major Solomon Van Rensselaer served for 40 years in public roles, as an eight-year veteran of the 1790s Army, New York militia leader, member of Congress and Postmaster in New York. Such examples abound; other officers served as justices, mayors, Indian agents, lawmen, and senior militia leaders, both before and after their military service. Such ties to civilian society were important, limiting the tendency to view officership as an isolated profession. Rather, officers tended to view military leadership as part of a larger societal leadership role. Arthur St. Clair's declaration that "no man has a right to withhold his services when his country needs them . . . Be the sacrifices ever so great, it must be yielded upon the altar of patriotism" evidently spoke for many military officers of the period.[47] St. Clair's example supported his words; he served 39 years in public service as county surveyor and local politician, Revolutionary War general, Confederation Congress member and president, and territorial secretary and governor.

Poor living conditions and meager prospects for increased pay and promotion and the temptation to leverage position for selfish advantage provided a significant challenge not just in the aftermath of defeat but throughout the period. In 1790, rumors circulated that several captains at Fort Knox had established stores for their own profit, providing credit to Soldiers while charging exorbitant prices for necessary goods and then withholding Soldiers' pay in payment. Senior leaders' response to such rumors indicates that these Army leaders understood the threat such actions posed to the principle of selfless service within the Army itself. Harmar condemned any such profiteering at Soldiers' expense, charging the post commander to immediately investigate such rumors and take action to stop any such "dishonorable speculation" and vowing, "if I find any officer is concerned in it, he shall be called to a strict and severe account for such unmilitary proceedings."[48]

The danger posed to honorable service by avarice and selfishness is especially evident in the extraordinary career of Major Butler's nemesis, General James Wilkinson.[49] A Revolutionary veteran and well-connected leader in Kentucky, Wilkinson gained a federal commission as a lieutenant colonel in 1792 and served as Wayne's senior regular officer until the latter's death in 1796. Dissatisfaction with his personal financial prospects led Wilkinson to secure a second career as a paid agent of Spain, in direct contradiction of his oath of office. By 1794, Wayne and senior government officials rightly suspected Wilkinson of a multitude of nefarious schemes placing himself and his prospects ahead of the good of the Army or the country, including the gathering of a coterie of officers in an attempt to undermine Wayne's authority. Called a "vile assassin" by Wayne and convincingly judged as the most "despicable character" in all of American history by Theodore Roosevelt, Wilkinson escaped conviction by a remarkable mix of cleverness, luck, and political connections.[50] As will be seen in the following chapter on esprit, Wilkinson's selfish service resulted in tremendous dissension within the officer corps, damaging attempts to establish a strong tradition of selfless service in the early republic's Army officer corps. A comprehensive study of the officer corps during Washington's presidency does reveal that Wilkinson was highly unusual in his absolute rejection of the concept of selfless service.

It is clear however, that strong obstacles impeded the early officer corps' development and practice of honorable selfless service. The young republic's shaky economic footing, coupled with continued ideological resistance to the establishment of a permanent professional officer corps even in the face of a dangerous Indian foe resulted in a largely unstable organizational foundation. Yet even in the midst of such instability and even under the negative influence of such unusual officers as Wilkinson, the early officer corps exhibited patterns of service generally characterized by strong and resilient commitment to the idea of sacrifice. This sacrificial service combined a readiness to die for the mission and for the country, even while demanding a healthy level of respect for the officer as an individual and for the officer corps as a body. Overwhelmingly committed to battlefield bravery and leading from the front, to enduring austere living conditions far from home, and to paternal-like service toward the enlisted soldier, most American Army officers between 1789 and 1796 served their new country with honor and commitment.

Notes

1. Headquarters, Department of the Army, ADP 1, sect. 2-18 and 2-19.

2. Headquarters, Department of the Army, *Whitepaper - Our Army Profession,* 8.

3. Thornbrough, *Outpost on the Wabash,* Harmar to Hamtramck, 20 February 1790, 221.

4. The correspondence of all three commanders reveal a near-constant shortage of basic supplies, as do such orderly books as those from Fort Knox and the diaries of such officers as Major Jonathon Heart, Captain Samuel Newman, Captain John Buell among others.

5. In multiple letters, Knox continuously stressed the need for paymasters to ensure accountability while Harmar, St. Clair, and Wayne repeatedly emphasized the need for on-time delivery of funds to pay Soldiers.

6. United States, *American State Papers, Indian Affairs*, Knox to Gaither, 17 July 1793, 367. Washington advised General Wayne a few months earlier to spend money only on "what is indispensably necessary to cover and service the Officers and Soldiers from the weather, avoiding all decorations, and as much as possible all conveniences." George Washington, "Observations on General Wayne's Letters," 23 November 1792, *The George Washington Papers,* Alderman Library, University of Virginia, Charlottesville, VA, 26 September 1796, http://gwpapers.virginia.edu (accessed 7 May 2013).

7. Gaff, 12.

8. Smith, *The St. Clair Papers*, Doughty to Major Wyllys, 25 March 1790, 134.

9. Thornbrough, *Outpost on the Wabash,* Melcher to Hamtramck, 28 July 1790, 238 and Hamtramck to Harmar, 15 June 1791, 283.

10. As described in previous chapters, most useful for a history of the campaigns and the actions of officers in combat are Sword and Gaff.

11. Underwood, 13.

12. Knox correspondence in United States, *American State Papers, Indian Affairs*, 234.

13. Sword, 113-114.

14. General Butler's ensuing death was a particularly gruesome one, with Indians tomahawking him and then opening his chest to take his heart before cutting it in pieces and sharing it to eat, apparently in order to capture the general's brave spirit. The brave death of Butler, and the bravery of other officers, is described in Jacob, 107-108.

15. Winthrop Sargent, *Diary of Colonel Winthrop Sargent, Adjutant General of the United States' Army, During the Campaign of 1791* (Wormsloe, GA: 1851), 68.

16. Statistics are drawn from the Army Adjutant General's count in Sargent, *Diary of Colonel Winthrop Sargent*, 260.

17. Jackson Johonnet, *The Remarkable Adventures of Jackson Johonnet of Massachusetts, Who Served as a Soldier in the Western Army, in the Massachusetts Line, in the Expedition under General Harmar, and the Unfortunate General St. Clair, Containing an Account of His Captivity, Sufferings, and Escape from the Kickapoo Indians* (Boston, MA: S. Hall, 1793), 15.

18. Harmar, *The Proceedings of a Court of Enquiry.*

19. Knopf, *Anthony Wayne*, Wayne to Knox, 15 January 1793, 171.

20. Skelton, *An American Profession of Arms*, 34-35.

21. Denny, 15.

22. Denny, 177.

23. Joseph M. Beatty, ed., "Letters of the Four Beatty Brothers," *Pennsylvania Magazine of History and Biography* 44, no. 3 (1920): 192-263.

24. Booraem, 159.

25. Booraem, 162.

26. Data gleaned from Heitman as well as Fredriksen.

27. Years of service calculated from officer biographical entries in Heitman.

28. George Washington, "Washington to Continental Congress," 29 January 1778, *The George Washington Papers,* Alderman Library, University of Virginia, Charlottesville, VA, 26 September 1796, http://gwpapers.virginia.edu (accessed 7 May 2013).

29. Gaff, Hamtramck to Harmar, 7 July 1793, 123.

30. Booraem, William Henry Harrison to brother, 27 November 1794, 109.

31. Detailed information on Major Butler was drawn from J. A. Murray, "The Butlers of Cumberland Valley," *Historical Register: Notes and Queries* I (January 1883); and J. A. Murray, "The Butler Family of the Pennsylvania Line" *The Pennsylvania Magazine of History and Biography* 7, no. 1 (1883): 1-6.

32. Murray, "The Butler Family of the Pennsylvania Line," 7.

33. The bizarre nature of this case was subjected to lampoon in a short story by Washington Irving entitled "General Von Poffenburgh."

34. Thornbrough, *Outpost on the Wabash,* Captain John Armstrong to Harmar, 29 December 1788, 143; and Harmar, *The Proceedings of a Court of Inquiry,* 27.

35. John Armstrong, *The John Armstrong Papers* (Indianapolis, IN: Indiana Historical Society, n.d.), Harmar to Armstrong, 28 July 1789.

36. The incorporation of Washington's vision into Steuben's understanding of drill, maneuver, and administration is convincingly described in Paul D. Lockhart, *The Drillmaster of Valley Forge: The Baron de Steuben and the Making of the American Army* (Washington, DC: Smithsonian, 2008), 169-196; Washington's influence on Revolutionary War officers is convincingly described in Higginbotham, *George Washington and the American Military Tradition.*

37. Steuben, 128, 135.

38. Steuben, 127-128.

39. Knopf, *Orderly Books of the United States Legion*, 16 August 1792, 11.

40. Knopf, *Anthony Wayne*, Wayne to Knox, 6 December 1792, 147-148.

41. Knopf, *Orderly Books of the United States Legion*, 16 August 1792, 11.

42. Guthman, 67; and Smith, *The St. Clair Papers*, St. Clair to Knox, 1 May 1790, 140.

43. Pay scales for the 1780s and 1790s are given in Guthman, 6, 145.

44. See, for instance, Knopf, *Orderly Books for the United States Legion;* Quaife, "Fort Knox Orderly Books."

45. Knopf, *Orderly Books for the United States Legion*, 9.

46. See for example, Huntington, Cunliffe, and Millett, *Military Professionalism and Officership in America.*

47. Wilson, *Arthur St. Clair*, St. Clair to James Wilkinson, 23.

48. Thornbrough, *Outpost on the Wabash,* Harmar to Captain James Bradford, 3 September 1790, 257; and Harmar to Hamtramck, 27 August 1790, 252-253. See also Denny, Harmar to Joseph Howell, 9 June 1890, 252-253.

49. The latest and most thorough account of Wilkinson's life is Andro Linklater, *An Artist in Treason: The Extraordinary Double Life of General James Wilkinson* (New York, NY: Walker Publishing, 2009).

50. Wayne' characterization is found in Richard Kohn, "General Wilkinson's Vendetta with General Wayne: Politics and Command in the American Army, 1791-1796" *The Filson Club Quarterly* 45, no. 4 (Fall, 1971): 366; Roosevelt's conclusion is in Theodore Roosevelt, *The Winning of the West, vol. III* (New York, NY: Putnam, 1889), 124.

Chapter 6
Military Professionalism and Esprit in the Early American Army Officer Corps, 1789 – 1796

The Army depicts esprit de corps as the fourth of the five characteristics central to military professionalism. According to this doctrinal manual, esprit provides a shared sense of purpose in the pursuit of the common goal of excellence, strong bonds of loyalty and pride, and a winning and disciplined spirit. It reflects the acceptance and internalization of the 'band of brothers' concept in which "spirited and dedicated professionals" are "bonded together in cohesive units and organizations."[1]

Esprit is grounded in a respect for the history and tradition of the Army and its mission and purpose, as well as in the shared experiences of Soldiers working and training together in an atmosphere of mutual respect. The Army's dedication to organizational customs, traditions, and ceremonies emphasizes and supports this shared respect for the Army's history and tradition. A positive command climate, characterized by candor, trust, and leader concern, supports the development of esprit within units. Finally, Army doctrine depicts esprit existing at multiple levels, including among small groups of individuals, within small elements and large units, and in the Army as a whole.[2]

This chapter describes the nature of esprit de corps in the early Army officer corps. It describes the character and quality of cohesion among officers within the Army, while also examining the way in which the officer corps relates to militia and volunteer forces. In doing so, this chapter discusses the way in which officers understood and practiced concepts of loyalty, pride, discipline, command climate, and respect, at both the team and larger organizational level.

Three general patterns emerge from this study of cohesion within the American officer corps during Washington's presidency. First, high levels of friendship, camaraderie and esprit frequently developed among small clusters of leaders and within sub-units and modest-sized organizations of officers. These small pockets of unified officers often shared a similar background, experience, or concern. Though limited, the presence of such clusters of officers sharing bonds of communal loyalty and pride was an important and positive element that promoted esprit and cohesion within the officer corps. Second, despite cohesion among clusters of officers, strong internal officer corps dissension and bickering developed as the Army expanded and the relatively harmonious group of officers that saw service under the Confederation, gave way to a much larger and more contentious body of officers by 1792. Officers' internal disputes threatened all attempts to inculcate an authentic sense of esprit and organizational and unit cohesion. Caused by a loss of widely shared formative experiences among younger officers and a series of divisive splits among senior officers, this dissension led to greater levels of instability and damaged officer corps esprit. Third, given the nature of the early American military establishment, the regular Army-militia relationship was of critical importance and provided a severe challenge to the regular Army officer corps, with high levels of distrust impeding any real esprit between regular and militia or volunteer forces. Between 1792 and 1794 however, a measured and limited sense of cohesion and esprit developed gradually, and to a limited extent, but that development and the successful use of a combined force was one of the most important aspects of the Northwest Indian War.

American officers emerged from the Revolutionary War with a general vision of their officer corps as a cohesive band of brothers-in-arms. Internal dissension and the formation of coteries of officers around powerful generals existed, yet the long years of war and the dramatic victory, coupled with a generally fervent devotion to their commanding general, resulted in a tight-knit group of officers with a high level of esprit. The founding of the Society of the Cincinnati in 1783 illustrates the overall unity within the officer corps. With over 350 founding members and state societies that rapidly included a majority of officers serving at the end of the war, the Society was both a vehicle to seek post-war compensation for their services and a way to express the esprit and camaraderie that the officer corps had formed during long years of service under General Washington.[3]

The small group of 44 officers that comprised the officer corps of 1789, inherited from the group of officers serving under the Articles of Confederation, consisted overwhelmingly of Revolutionary War veterans and most had served together for at least several years in the late 1780s.[4] General Harmar seems to have done little to explicitly target a continued sense of esprit, but with a group of officers who largely shared a powerful formative foundation, perhaps there seemed little need to focus particularly on esprit among federal officers. Available journals, orderly books and other correspondence indicate few instances of dissension or conflict within this officer corps and a substantial evidence of a shared commitment to group values and loyalty. For instance, most demonstrated some sense of communal pride and cohesion by membership in the Society of the Cincinnati.[5] High levels of trust, respect and loyalty are very evident in the correspondence between Harmar and most of his officers. For example, a series of letters between June 1790 and January 1791, involving rumors of officer speculation using government funds, is impressive for the candor and respect it displays among such long-time Revolutionary and Confederation comrades as General Harmar and Majors Hamtramck and Wyllys.[6] Letters between Captain John Armstrong, Hamtramck and Harmar point to a high level of confidence, dedication to the mission, and trust in one another, resulting in an evident strong level of esprit.[7] Perhaps the most telling indicator of a high level of esprit occurred in the aftermath of Harmar's disappointing 1790 campaign, for which he was relieved of command. In his 1791 court of inquiry, the investigating board called 15 of his officers to testify; every single one of them professed great respect, loyalty and confidence in their former commanding officer and the campaign's goal of punishing hostile Indian tribes.[8] Harmar's small group of officers certainly suffered some internal dissension. Majors Hamtramck and John Doughty disputed over rank throughout the 1780s until 1789 when the War Department definitely ruled on their dates of rank, but in general, evidence indicates a high level of cohesion, sense of shared purpose, and esprit among the small group of federal officers in 1789.[9]

A strong sense of esprit also prospered among slightly smaller clusters of officers throughout this period. For instance, an especially high level of cohesion existed among a small number of mostly cavalry officers serving in General Wayne's Legion. Existing letters between Captains Solomon Van Rensselaer, Edward Turner, John Webb, and Robert MisCampbell and Lieutenants Campbell Smith and Nanning Vissher reveal a tightly knit band of junior officers.[10] One 1794 exchange between Captain Rensselaer and Lieutenant Vissher shows a particularly powerful sense of camaraderie and a shared dedication to duty. Writing with black and characteristic humor on the eve of the campaign's decisive battle, Vissher asked Rensselaer to "inform me whether you have yet had an opportunity of slashing with temporary advantages; if not, I hope you soon may, and that you may even be honorably killed!! To hear of your death would be a good story for me to carry home, and would so well please all your friends."[11] Rensselaer's playful yet poignant response two days after the battle, addressed to "my dear Van Munickhousen," informs his friend of the battle, including news of his serious chest wound. Rensselaer asks Vissher to avoid alarming friends by telling them of the wound, noting that if he does die, he hopes others "will not repine at my lot, as I will die in the arms of victory and in a glorious cause." Rensselaer concludes with news of the death of their fellow friend: "the gallant Campbell is no More; perhaps I shall soon lay with him in the grave. My aged Parents will grieve. Adieu, Adieu my dear Vissher, may you be well and happy is the wish (and perhaps the last one) of your sincere friend."[12] Captain MisCampbell's will, executed upon his death mentioned here, included a provision stating, "My Silver Hilted Sword I give to my beloved friend Capt. Soln. Van Rensselaer in confidence that he will never disgrace it."[13] Rensselaer's reaction to his life-threatening wound suffered at Fallen Timbers reveals this developing pride in the cavalry branch and in the officer corps. Questioned for his refusal to resort to a stretcher to depart the field, the 20-year-old dragoon officer proudly declared, "I am an officer of the cavalry, and shall go on horseback."[14] The interactions between these six junior officers reveal a spirited and dedicated service, founded at least in part upon a resilient small-group esprit de corps.

The relatively common tendency of families developing a tradition of officer service also provided an immediate infusion of small-group camaraderie. The Butler family of Pennsylvania is probably the most striking example of this. After five sons of the family served as officers in the Revolutionary War, General Richard Butler, Major Thomas Butler, and Captain Edward Butler continued to serve together in the Northwest Indian War. In addition, nephew Lieutenant Richard Butler served as a staff officer under Wayne. During the 1791 defeat at the hands of the Indian confederation, Edward saved the life of the severely wounded Thomas.[15] A brief perusal of officer lists during Washington's presidency reveals at least 13 families with close relatives serving together in the federal officer corps.[16] In a small body of officers, such family member groups and their associates within the young officer corps provided important clusters likely to have high levels of esprit and a shared sense of purpose and service.

At an even lower level, strong friendships between officers sharing a sense of dedication to the mission provided an important and productive esprit within the officer corps. The shared experiences and dangers that challenged officers on the frontier led to influential and resilient friendships that promoted powerful bonds of loyalty and respect. For example, Lieutenant William Clark's bonds of friendship with fellow officers exemplified this common dynamic. While commanding a rifle company in 1795, Clark met newly commissioned Ensign Meriwether Lewis. Sharing a Virginia Piedmont boyhood, avidity for adventure, and an obvious interest in military affairs, the two developed a strong friendship founded on respect and affection. When tasked by President Jefferson to explore the west in 1803, Captain Lewis turned to his friend, asking Clark to co-lead the exploring party. Their strong and professionally constructive relationship continued to bear fruit after the famous expedition; in 1807, Lewis resigned from the Army to take the governorship of the new Louisiana Territory and he asked Clark to share his St. Louis headquarters as the head of the territorial militia. Letters between Clark and Lewis throughout this period reveal an intimate friendship, further evident in the name chosen for Clark's eldest son: Meriwether Lewis Clark. Clark's close friendship with another veteran Legion officer, Captain Peter Grayson, led to Clark's marriage to Grayson's sister-in-law in 1808.[17]

Similar strong friendships appear often within the officer corps, built on shared experiences and camaraderie. For instance, Lieutenant Cornelius Sedan and Captain David Ziegler served together under Wayne, resulting in a lifetime friendship testified to by the name of Sedan's future son, David Zeigler Sedan.[18] Lieutenant William H. Harrison's friendship with Winthrop Sargent began with their common service as officers in 1792 and continued throughout the decade, resulting in Harrison earning Sargent's recommendation and then job, succeeding his friend as territorial secretary in 1798.[19]

One last representative example reveals the type and existence of small-group cohesion so important to the officer corps' development as a resilient force, while at the same time providing a sense of the internal dissension that threatened esprit across the corps as a whole. Surgeon Mate Joseph Andrews maintained a gossipy diary during his assignment as one of a group of eight officers at Fort Defiance in 1795. One of Andrews' favorite topics concerns food, and his diary entries frequently note the officers of the garrison trading and combining their culinary fare. His depiction of Christmas day festivities in 1795 includes a description of an all-day convivial gathering among the officers, focusing on smoking and the sharing of duck, raccoon, pudding, jellies, chicken, squirrels, rabbit, and venison as well as apple toddies and whiskey.[20] Andrews describes the fort's officers continually dining together, banding together to buy barrels of cider and hospital stores to replace needed supplies and of collaborating in a "co-partnership to manufacture maple sugar."[21] This and his depiction of the officers' sorrowful and communal reaction to the death of an unnamed ensign in 1795 indicates a real sense of community and shared reaction to the challenges of serving in an isolated garrison.[22]

Thus, while primary sources reveal strong bonds between small groups of officers, the same documents often evince an extensive number of officer disputes that threatened to poison relations in the officer corps and overwhelm the small building blocks of esprit demonstrated in the previous pages. The diary of Surgeon Mate Andrews reveals the way in which this small community of officers grappled with internal tensions that posed such a threat to the early officer corps' esprit. In late 1795, Andrews relates that Major Thomas Cushing and Lieutenant Piercy Pope quarreled for an unspecified reason, threatening accord among the post's officers. In response, the remaining officers present, Major Thomas Hunt, Captain Bernard Gaines, Ensign George Strother and Andrews, intervened and reconciled the disputants.[23] Such reconciliations were required startlingly often due to the ongoing problem of disputes between officers. A diary entry from another Legion officer, Lieutenant Boyer, describes a recurring experience: "Lieutenant Blue of the dragoons was this day arrested by ensign Johnson of the 4th Sub Legion, but a number of their friends interfering the dispute was settled upon Lieutenant Blue's asking Ensign Johnson's pardon."[24] While most officer disputes ended peacefully, often through the successful interventions of other officers, sometimes disputes escalated with a corrosive effect on officer corps esprit.

This was particularly true of the officer corps in Wayne's Legion, between 1792 and 1796, in which according to Major Buell's journal entry for 23 February 1793, "there was the most quarreling . . . throughout the whole legion that I ever knew in any army."[25] Multiple primary sources support this claim, recording over 15 duels fought between officers in 1793-1794 alone.[26] During this time, the officer corps rapidly expanded and a large number of young officers entered the service, without the shared experiences that characterized older officers bonded by service during the Revolutionary War or Confederation era. This likely had a heavy influence on the significant increase in the number of officer disputes in Wayne's officer corps. Without a foundation of past cohesion or shared experiences, these young officers allowed minor disputes to escalate into violence. Buell recorded the details of a duel that killed both participants, Lieutenant Nathaniel Huston and Lieutenant John Bradshaw, noting that the two fought over a petty dispute when the latter was drunk.[27] At least four officers of the Legion died in duels, with others wounded and many more involved in duels settled or fought without injury.[28] The practice of dueling by itself, especially those decided without serious injury, may not have been as deadly to esprit as it likely appears at first glance, for there was consensus that a limited amount of dueling served a useful and honorable service.[29] General Wayne had ambiguous feelings about the practice, seeing it as a way to avoid time-consuming courts-martials, while lamenting the toll it took on his officers, especially those of junior status.[30]

A backdrop of bitter and divisive splits among senior officers however, invested officer duels and other disputes with a special intensity and partisan character which threatened to corrode the developing sense of esprit throughout the officer corps. In fact, the caustic relationship that developed between the two senior regular officers in the Legion, Generals Wayne and Wilkinson, was behind much of the tension and discord that is so strikingly evident within the Legion's officer corps. Bitterly disappointed after being passed over for the job of commanding general in 1792, the ambitious and ever-unscrupulous Wilkinson immediately schemed to undermine and replace Wayne. As part of his multi-pronged plan to do so, Wilkinson castigated Wayne to political allies, wrote anonymous letters to newspapers charging Wayne with incompetence and ignorance, and gathered officers like Major Cushing, Captain Isaac Guion, and Lieutenant Clark into his anti-Wayne camp. Wilkinson openly condemned Wayne to these officers throughout the Fallen Timbers campaign, complaining to them about Wayne's arrogance, favoritism, and unwillingness to listen to his ideas.[31]

Such actions bore divisive fruit among officers. Clark served under General Wilkinson upon his entry to the Legion in 1792 and quickly succumbed to his superior's campaign to discredit Wayne. At the very most decisive point of the Fallen Timbers campaign, Clark's journal reveals the consequences of such machinations by Wilkinson. Noting that Wayne had ignored Wilkinson's recommendation to forsake his slow and systematic advance for a sudden strike against the Miami Indian villages, Clark angrily condemned Wayne and his supporters who "forego such opportunities of rendering their Country a service and absolutely so far neglect their duty."[32] In the available orderly books recording the recurring disputes between officers, one notes that usually each disputant belonged to one of these two rival camps. Officers like Cushing, Guion, and Lieutenant Blue clashed with pro-Wayne officers like Major Buell, Major Thomas Doyle, and Captain John Webb. All evidence supports the 1795 diary record of Surgeon Mate Andrews that most officers assumed that Wilkinson had "endeavored to raise a party in opposition to the Commander in Chief." Such actions resulted in a situation where "there was no expression more common than such an officer in is favor of Wayne; such a one in favor of Wilkinson."[33]

It is difficult to overstate the damage done by Wilkinson to the overall state of cohesion among Army officers. A brief letter from Lieutenant Blue to Captain Van Rensselaer is a final powerful example of the damage done to officer unity and sense of shared purpose by Wilkinson's habit of supporting favored officers while denigrating others. After a dispute of some kind with his commanding officer, Major William Winston, Blue crowed to his fellow officer "the Major and his friendship may both go to hell. I have a better, a more powerful and a more confidential friend in my General (Wilkinson), and while I can maintain his good will, I feel easy . . ."[34]

In addition to corrupting cohesion within the officer corps, Wilkinson's actions pushed out veteran and competent officers with strong ties to others in the officer corps and who had revealed a dedication to the Army's mission and to a professional development of esprit. For example, Captain John Armstrong refused to join the anti-Wayne cabal gathered around Wilkinson. In return, Wilkinson pushed Armstrong out of the Army in 1793, on trumped up charges designed to embarrass both Armstrong and Wayne.[35] Thus because of Wilkinson's bad influence, the Army lost a Revolutionary War veteran with over 16 years of service to the nation and with an outstanding record of achievement. Similarly, Revolutionary War veteran Major David Ziegler resigned his commission in 1792 after he tired of Wilkinson's "schemes and machinations."[36]

This situation, so obviously damaging to cohesion within the officer corps, persisted until Wayne's death in 1796. One of the greatest failures of the Washington administration's oversight of the Army was a failure to resolve the tension created by this divide amongst senior officers. Well aware of the rancor between Wayne and Wilkinson by 1794, the failure by Washington and Knox to take decisive action to resolve such divides will be examined in the next chapter on stewardship, for it not only impacted the esprit of the officer corps but also its long-term health.

Never able to fully overcome the heavy internal dissension that bedeviled the officer corps during his four-year command, General Wayne experienced greater success in instilling a generally confident and winning spirit among his officers. In fact, the development of a 'winning spirit' advocated by *The Army* was one of the greatest achievements of the officer corps during the latter half of Washington's term. This accomplishment was especially important in the face of two disheartening Army failures under Generals Harmar and St. Clair.

Before St. Clair's campaign in 1791, Harmar represented the lack of confidence and defeatism shared by many when he urged Lieutenant Denny not to resign but urged, "You must go on the campaign; some will escape, and you may be among the number."[37] As St. Clair's offensive pushed forward amidst crippling logistical, intelligence and regular-militia relationship issues, the sense of unease shared by numerous officers only deepened.[38] Several years later, Wayne fought hard to avoid such defeatism and to promote unit pride, camaraderie and a sense of shared purpose in accomplishing the mission. Unlike Harmar, commanding a generally cohesive body of officers, and St. Clair, leading an officer corps on such a short timeline that it seems there was little time for real attention to the development of officer esprit, Wayne had the need, time and inclination to comprehensively tackle esprit development by focusing on individual and unit pride, discipline and cohesion.

Soon after taking command, Wayne collaborated with Secretary Knox to devise distinctive markings for his newly organized Legion. Each of the four sub-legions received white, red, yellow, or black hat bindings with similarly colored plumes, and a Legionary standard and sub-legionary colors were devised and delivered to the Army.[39] The training regimen instituted by Wayne included a heavy focus on building sub-unit bonds and camaraderie, offering rewards (usually in the form of an extra ration of whiskey) for top shooting marksmen and small groups. Wayne even had a fives court (similar to a handball court) built for officers, to promote esprit.[40] Continually reiterating that officers must be decisively engaged in training to build trust, Wayne sought to build confidence among officers and across the Legion as a whole.[41] Through strong improvements in discipline, training, intelligence, and regular-militia coordination and slight logistical improvements, Legion officers soon developed a shared sense of confidence. Journals and correspondence prior to Fallen Timbers records this new belief and sense of self-assurance. On the eve of the battle, Captain William Eaton asserted with representative confidence, "we are well disciplined and well reconciled to the expedition, and whatever may be our success, I will venture to assure you, that we shall not fly."[42]

The third key development concerning esprit and cohesion within the officer corps in the early Army involves the relationship between regular and militia or volunteer forces. As noted in the previous thesis chapter on trust, senior national leaders fully accepted that non-regular forces (defined as militia or volunteer organizations) were central to military operations. All significant operations across the frontier during Washington's presidency were either combined efforts with regular and non-regular units or conducted exclusively by militia or volunteers. This reality habitually forced federal officers to coordinate operations with non-regular units. Unfortunately from the very beginning, there was a tremendous lack of cohesion between the federal officer corps and other military forces, limiting the effectiveness of the combined force's operations during the Harmar and St. Clair campaigns.

From the perspective of the federal officers perspective, this lack of cohesion resulted from a near absolute lack of trust in the militia and volunteers. Officers' scorn for the militia emanated from regular officers' correspondence. Such notes from officers consistently decried the state forces' amateurism, lack of dedication, and unwillingness to sacrifice. Harmar's representative statement to Captain Armstrong in 1789 that "no person can hold a more contemptible opinion of the militia than I do" indicates how a concern for esprit and cohesion among Harmar's officers was limited to federal officers and not the combined military establishment.[43] Similarly, federal officers serving under General St. Clair evinced scant regard for any sense of the need for esprit or cohesion between their forces and the militia units involved in the campaign. St. Clair himself bitterly castigated the efforts of militia forces, largely blaming them for the Army's rout.[44] Regular officers like Major Sargent and Captain Armstrong blamed militia cowardice and incompetence for the defeat, vowing never again to serve with such non-regular elements.[45] It is evident that the almost visceral reaction of many regular officers to the obvious weakness of militia organizations blinded officers to the fact that effective combined operations, so necessary given the nature of the country's military establishment, cried out for serious attention to the development of some level of regular and militia cooperation.

Another of General Wayne's important accomplishments was his recognition and management of this reality. As wide-eyed as his predecessors, Wayne recognized the many weaknesses of non-regular forces and imposed directives to account for these and to limit corrosive consequences to the Army's overall esprit. In a strongly worded letter to Secretary Knox, Wayne refused to operate with either militia or volunteer elements unless all parties clearly accepted that Wayne was the commander in chief of all American forces in the offensive, with non-regulars being fully "amenable to my orders and directions."[46] Unlike previous campaigns where command authority of the regular Army commander relating to state forces was ambiguous, Washington and Knox ensured that in the Fallen Timbers campaign, there was no doubt that in Knox's words, "every part of the arrangements is under your (Wayne's) control."[47] At the same time, Wayne acknowledged the particular worth of the Kentucky mounted volunteers that combined with regular units to form the American Army in 1794. In fact, Wayne successfully lobbied Washington and Knox to name the commander of the 1,500 Kentucky volunteers, Major General Charles Scott, as the combined Army's second in command, ahead of all other regular Army officers. The high level of respect, esprit and determination shared by Wayne and Scott is evident and formed an important ingredient in the much improved nature of the coordination and common pursuit of the overall goal. Scott was an experienced veteran of the French and Indian War and the American Revolution and shared with Wayne the experience of serving as a brigade commander under Washington. The resulting sense of trust and respect between these commanders, one a regular and one a state officer, highlights the possibility afforded by shared service.[48]

Wayne's integration of the militia into the scheme of operations, to a much greater extent than had been done under the two previous Army commanders, further indicates his acceptance of the importance of effective cohesion and cooperation. Employing the Kentuckians as spies, scouts, supply escorts, screens, reserves, and a counterattacking force, Wayne and Scott integrated regular and volunteer units as had not happened since the Revolution.[49] Perhaps most indicative of the vastly improved dynamic between regular and non-regular forces and their leaders is Wayne's General Order of 28 August 1794. This order stated, "the commander-in-chief wishes it to be fairly understood that when he mentioned or may mention the Federal army in general orders, that term comprehends and includes the legion and mounted volunteers as one compound army."[50] Complaints by federal officers about the capability and spirit of non-regular forces remained, but for the first time in the United States Army, regular and non-regular forces performed combined large-scale operations in an effective manner. There is no doubt that regular Army officers followed Wayne's lead and recognized this; primary sources during the Fallen Timbers campaign are far more complimentary to non-regulars and their leaders than in past campaigns.[51]

George Washington and Henry Knox insisted throughout the 1780s and 1790s that combined operations with regulars and well-trained and led militia or volunteers could form a basis for an effective American military establishment. In light of the failures of 1790 and 1791, this claim was often doubted until it was validated by Wayne's decisive victory at Fallen Timbers. Supported by General Scott, Wayne's dedication to cohesion across the entire force and the victory of Fallen Timbers thus validated Washington's vision and was therefore one of the most profound of Wayne's contributions to the early American military tradition.

Thus, the early American officer corps experienced tremendous challenges in developing authentic cohesion and esprit. Officer disputes, founded upon a sensitive regard for personal honor, an increasing number of junior officers without a shared experience in past conflicts, and especially divisive conflict between senior officers, resulted in a failure to establish a high sense of shared loyalty or purpose across the officer corps as a whole. At the same time, officers did develop and demonstrate substantial camaraderie, a shared commitment to mission and a communal sense of loyalty and unit pride. As might be expected, this was especially true among officers sharing profound experiences of some kind. Towards the latter part of Washington's presidency, Army leaders increasingly focused on improving cohesion within the military establishment, and regular and non-regular military leaders made substantial strides toward more cohesive relations. These actions targeted increased levels of esprit as well as positive stewardship, the topic of the next chapter.

Notes

1. Headquarters, Department of the Army, *Whitepaper - Our Army Profession,* 11.

2. Headquarters, Department of the Army, ADP 1, sect. 2-20 to 2-24.

3. Data on the Society and the Cincinnati and its members was drawn primarily from primary sources in the first two boxes of the "Proceedings of the General Society of the Cincinnati, 1783-1902," Society of Cincinnati's Headquarters, Washington DC; as well as from Minor Myers, *Liberty without Anarchy: A History of the Society of the Cincinnati* (Charlottesville, VA: University of Virginia Press, 1983).

4. Identifying all 44 of these officers is difficult, yet a fairly comprehensive list can be gathered by combining lists found in Heitman, various lists found in United States, *American State Papers, Military Affairs*, and the journal kept by Harmar's adjutant, Denny, in his *Military Journal.*

5. It appears from society rosters (see footnote 243 above for sources) that over 20 of the original 44 1789 officers were founding members of the society, with more joining later in the 1780s.

6. Series of letters between the three on this topic commences with a letter from Hamtramck to Harmar on 24 June 1790 and ends on 25 January 1791. During this time, Harmar's force suffered its defeat with the loss of many men including several officers, causing Hamtramck to note to Harmar that "I very lament the loss of so many men but particularly that of my excellent friend Wyllys," (2 December 1790). These letters are printed in Thornbrough, *Outpost on the Wabash Letters*, 235-276.

7. Letters between these officers are found loose in Armstrong and Thornbrough, *Outpost on the Wabash Letters*, 173–198.

8. Testimony given throughout Harmar, *The Proceedings of a Court of Inquiry*.

9. Correspondence between Knox, Harmar, and Captain Bradshaw in 1789 indicates this dispute over rank; see letters in Thornbrough, *Outpost on the Wabash Letters*, 164-165.

10. Series of letters between these officers in 1794 and 1795 is reprinted in Catharina Vissher Bonney, *A Legacy of Historical Gleanings* I (Albany, NY: J. Munsell, 1875), 96-146.

11. Bonney, Vissher to Rensselaer, 1 August 1794, 101.

12. Bonney, Rensselaer to Vissher, 22 August 1794, 104.

13. Bonney, Captain MisCampbell's will, 102.

14. Bonney.

15. Murray, "The Butler Family of the Pennsylvania Line," 1-6.

16. There are likely others, but families with relatives serving together include the Butlers, Harrisons, Poseys, Pikes, Smiths, Strothers, Bradys, Graysons, Mills, Bissells, Freemans, Sloughs and Strongs.

17. The continuing influence of Clark's Army officer friendships is evident throughout Jones.

18. Emma Backus, "Cornelius Sedam and his Friends in Washington's Time," *Ohio Archaeological and Historical Quarterly* 41, no. 1 (January 1932): 44.

19. Booraem, 86, 165.

20. Knopf, *A Surgeon's Mate at Fort Defiance*, 65.

21. Knopf, 54, 45, 14.

22. Knopf, 52.

23. Knopf, *A Surgeon's Mate at Fort Defiance*, 50.

24. Lieutenant Boyer, *A Journal of Wayne's Campaign. Being an Authenthic Daily Record of the Most Important Occurrences During the Campaign of Major General Anthony Wayne, against the Northwestern Indians* (Cincinnati, OH: Printed for W. Dodge by J. F. Uhlhorn, 1866), 18. The word "arrest" meant in this context not necessarily a legal action but a reproof or challenge to provide redress of some sort for a perceived act of wrongdoing, injustice or insult.

25. John Hutchinson Buell, *The Diary of John Hutchison Buell*, ed. Richard Knopf (Columbus, OH: Anthony Wayne Parkway Board, Ohio State Museum, 1957), 5.

26. Both Lieutenant William Henry Harrison and Major John Buell record at least 15 duels fought, most without casualties, during 1793 and 1794. For Harrison's claim, see Booraem, 109; for Buell's claim, see Buell, 5.

27. Buell, 5.

28. Gaff; Ensign William Gassaway, Lieutenant Huston, Lieutenant John Bradshaw and Lieutenant George Dunn were four Legion officers known to have been killed via duel.

29. The practice of dueling demonstrates the continued tension within the officer corps between a high sense of personal honor and a dedication to honorable service as a military officer. For instance Lieutenant William Harrison's acceptance of dueling as a useful social practice was relatively common and accepted; Booraem.

30. The Army's Articles of War made dueling illegal and punishable but no legal action was taken against those generally viewed as taking part in a legitimate and sometimes necessary activity of honor. Wayne himself seems to have condoned dueling, noting in his orderly book in June, 1793 that "some other mode than of a general court martial" should settle personal disputes. Knopf, *Orderly Books of the US Legion*, 58.

31. While evident throughout available primary sources, the most succinct and useful summary of the bitter divide between Wayne and Wilkinson is Kohn, "General Wilkinson's Vendetta with General Wayne," 361-372.

32. Clark, 425.

33. Knopf, *A Surgeon's Mate at Fort Defiance,* 55.

34. Bonney, Blue to Rensselaer, 21 May 96, 123.

35. See Kohn, "General Wilkinson's Vendetta with General Wayne," 363, as well as documents in Armstrong.

36. George A. Katzenberger, "Major David Ziegler," *Ohio Archaeological and Historical Quarterly* 21 (April-July 1912): 156.

37. Denny, Harmar 25 September 1791 journal entry, 153.

38. Lieutenant Colonel Sargent, Captain Newman and Lieutenant Denny make this very clear in their individual journal entries in the weeks prior to the battle fought on 4 November 1791.

39. Knopf, *Anthony Wayne*, Knox to Wayne, 27 July 1792 and Wayne to Knox, 30 March 1793, 51, 212.

40. Booraem, 139.

41. Gaff, 62-63.

42. Captain Eaton quoted in Gaff, 156. Other officers' journals noting confidence on the eve of the battle included those of Lieutenant Clark and Lieutenant Boyer.

43. Thornbrough, *Outpost on the Wabash,* Harmar to Armstrong, 28 July 1789, 345.

44. United States, *American State Papers, Indian Affairs*, 136.

45. Reactions to St. Clair's defeat are recorded in Kohn, *Eagle and Sword,* 114-115.

46. Knopf, *Anthony Wayne*, Wayne to Knox, 20 June 1793, 244-245.

47. Knopf., Knox to Wayne, 16 May 1794, 329.

48. For Scott's extensive service as an officer, see Harry Ward, *Charles Scott and the Spirit of '76* (Charlottesville, VA: University of Virginia Press, 1988); see also Nelson, "General Charles Scott, the Kentucky Volunteers, and the Northwest Indian Wars, 1784-1794," 245. Wilkinson's unsurprising reaction to being passed over by Scott was to mount an attack on the Kentuckian, calling him a "fool, a scoundrel, and a poltroon."

49. Two good accounts of the integration of regulars and volunteers under Wayne are Millett, "Caesar and the Northwest: The Wayne Campaign, 1792-1795," 2-21 and Gaff.

50. General Order copied in Boyer, 11.

51. Several federal officer journals evince substantial respect for General Scott and many of his officers.

Chapter 7
Military Professionalism and Stewardship in the Early American Army Officer Corps, 1789 – 1796

Stewardship of the profession of arms is the fifth and final characteristic demanded of the military professional according to *The Army*. Professionals act as stewards of the Army by focusing on building "a better Army for tomorrow."[1]

Leaders accomplish this by protecting and promoting authentic trust, expertise, service and esprit in order to ensure the long-term effectiveness and health of the Army and the military profession. Through stewardship, professionals safeguard a long-term relationship with American society consistent with national values. Critical to stewardship is the self-regulation of members of the profession and a focus on leader development. Stewardship, according to Army doctrine, ensures disciplined development of Army professionals and leaders with the requisite competence, commitment, and character to apply land combat power while "exemplifying the ideals espoused by our ethos."[2]

This chapter describes the nature of stewardship in the early American officer corps between 1789 and 1796. Included is a description of the way leaders of the early military establishment understood stewardship and the strong challenges the environment of the 1790s presented to effective long-term care of the Army's corporate leadership. This discussion depicts officers' responses to these challenges and the resulting patterns of stewardship that developed within the officer corps. In seeking to shape the future Army and officer corps amidst these conditions, officers emphasized the importance of personal leadership, self-regulation and discipline of the officer corps, and an intimate connection among character, leadership, and stewardship. Convinced that only officers practiced the profession of arms, leaders of the early Army focused stewarding efforts on officers.[3]

Powerful challenges to an authentic sense of officer corps stewardship faced leaders between 1789 and 1796. First, the very real danger of an active and enterprising enemy along the northwest frontier and the need to garrison frontier posts preoccupied the Army and its officer corps. Throughout this period, and especially until the Treaty of Greeneville in 1796, combat operations and near-constant irregular warfare dominated Army efforts; this operational focus limited opportunities for the development of a long-term strategy for stewardship. Attempts to shape the future officer corps often quickly met the reality of a severe shortage of resources. For example, requests for federal forces along the southwest frontier went largely unmet until 1795 due to the Army's heavy focus on the Northwest Indian War.[4] Though leaders in the war department sought to shelter young officers slated to attend the fledgling artillery and engineering school at West Point in 1795, General Wayne's request for all available officers and the need to garrison forts finally vacated by the British in 1796, eventually stripped the school of its instructors and students.[5] Operating in an environment of tight fiscal constraints and in the face of a dangerous foe, this representative example demonstrates the officer corps' tendency to forsake long-term stewardship through education in favor of short-term execution of pressing and demanding missions.

Second, the organization and officer corps quickly and frequently swelled in accordance with the demands of wartime conflict; contraction was also a significant threat throughout this period, with congressional attempts to decrease the size, cost, and influence of the Army. In 1792 for instance, Congress attempted to undo the recent expansion of the Army, with a derogatory impact on officers' sense of stewardship.[6] Wayne reported that such attempts demoralized his officer corps, forcing them to consider that their efforts and sacrifice might not endure, and thus many officers, upon learning of such attempts, lose all "interest or pride in the discipline or appearance of their men."[7] Thus, officers' sense of responsibility toward the Army seemed to weaken in the face of uncertainty over both the Army's future and their own place within the organization. Additionally, senior Army leaders, so important to stewardship, changed frequently, undermining that stability that seems so conducive to charting a steady course for the future. General Harmar's command of the United States Army lasted less than two years, while General St. Clair served as commanding general for only about one year. General Wayne's four-year command offered the Army for the first time a stable and relatively long-serving chief. Unfortunately, the internal officer dissension discussed in the previous chapter, ongoing attempts to decrease the size of the Army and its officer corps, and a steady turnover in field grade officers threatened the establishment and implementation of a clear vision for long-term Army and officer corps development.

A third challenge to effective stewardship involved the fact that throughout this era officers were scattered in small numbers across a great swath of territory, ranging from the Great Lakes to the Georgia frontier, with a few sprinkled along the eastern seaboard. In 1789, the officer corps served at nine forts, primarily along the frontier. Three years later, officers served at 14 posts, with staff sizes ranging from two at Fort Fayette and Fort Steuben to nine at Fort Washington. By 1796, due to construction and assumption of posts vacated by British troops, federal officers staffed 19 posts. The three major campaigns of 1790, 1791, and 1793-1794 offered most of the Army an opportunity to interact as a whole, but a majority of an officer's time was spent at largely isolated outposts with only a limited number of officers. While major posts like Fort Washington held a substantial number of officers, the majority of garrisons held fewer than five officers. Focused on particular duties in a garrison far from other Army posts or officers, it was difficult to develop a real long-term plan for stewarding the profession.[8]

Fourth, the lack of institutional means by which a sense of stewardship might be nourished handicapped the officer corps. The aforementioned 1795 military school at West Point failed to develop until the following decade; all officer training continued to be on-the-job, received upon arrival to the assigned unit. Without a general staff and with a war department consisting of a staff which never rose above a total of seven officials during Washington's administration, the Army as an institution lacked depth. This jeopardized all attempts to implement Army-wide structural programs for the long-term good of the officer corps.[9]

Finally, the tremendous partisanship developed toward the latter half of the 1790s spilled over into the officer corps, with Wilkinson successfully seeking powerful political allies to promote his agenda of undermining the Federalist-leaning Wayne and his allies. Because of this, political calculations by leaders tended to compete with just demands for accountability. By 1795, the president and his administration were aware of Wilkinson's self-serving schemes, yet without hard proof, chose to ignore his behavior in hopes of avoiding the political fallout any prosecution of the general would likely incur.[10] From the very beginning of the nation, political pressures and calculations sometimes trumped the need for principled stewardship of the profession. Despite all these strong challenges, Army leaders did what they believed possible to ensure the long-term effectiveness of the Army officer corps and the Army profession, developing some vital patterns of stewardship during the first years of the republic.

At the very heart of officers' conceptions of stewardship was the realization that officers needed to reflect and perpetuate the values of the American republic, in order to ensure the long-term trustworthiness of the Army. Seeking to avoid the abuse of power so inimical to the fundamental American values of liberty and equal justice under the law, senior leaders emphasized officer accountability and adherence to selfless service. President Washington's influence seems especially powerful here;

he consistently emphasized to his subordinates that officers failing to live up to a decent standard of character and behavior set an insidious example that threatened the long-term health and trustworthiness of the officer corps. Throughout the Revolution, he insisted to his officers that leaders set a strong example, arguing, "when Officers set good Examples, it may be expected that the Men will with zeal and alacrity follow them . . . nor can they (officers) with any kind of propriety, or good Conscience, set in Judgment upon a Soldier for disobeying an order, which they themselves are everyday breaking."[11] As commanding general of the Continental Army, Washington consistently stressed the relationship between perceived character failings and an inability to fulfill the high calling of a leader, dismissing officers for drunkenness, perjury, slander, being absent without leave, refusing duties, homosexual acts, and cowardice.[12] As president, Washington directed his Army leaders to continue dismissing officers for such issues, advising Wayne in 1792, "so long as the vice of drunkenness exists in the Army so long I hope ejections of those Officers who are found guilty will continue, for that and gaming will debilitate and render unfit for active service any army whatever."[13] The president's example of demanding professional accountability, demonstrated by his swift removal from command of Harmar and St. Clair in the aftermath of their campaign failures, sent a powerful message to his senior Army leaders.

Leaders of the early Army took such guidance seriously, filling their orderly books and correspondence with records of officer punishment and dismissals as they sought to implement accountability across the officer corps. Commanding officers seemed especially intent upon quashing the development of aggrandizement based on position or rank. The unprincipled use of power over time threatened to lead to a sense of officer entitlement – the very opposite of the ideal of selfless service so critical to Army trustworthiness and long-term effectiveness and organizational health. For instance, hearing rumors of a leader at Fort Franklin employing Soldiers on the officer's personal business, General Harmar sent a terse note to Ensign John Jeffers at Fort Franklin that he was disappointed to hear that in the past, Soldiers at the post had been "almost continually employed on fatigue, and principally for (the officer's) own private emolument . . . Such conduct is a disgrace to the regiment, and any officer acting in like manner in future, shall be called to a severe account for it."[14]

A focus on developing accountability in the officer corps was especially evident in the Legion, as Wayne concentrated his efforts on incorporating Washington's emphasis on discipline as a critical component of shaping the future force. An examination of the Legion's orderly books reveals a constant grappling with issues of officer misconduct and strenuous efforts to dismiss the worst offenders while reprimanding those considered worthy of another opportunity. In the summer of 1792, Wayne approved the dismissal of Captain John Platt from the Army for drunkenness and conduct unbecoming an officer and gentleman, noting it was a senior officer's duty "not to permit such unworthy conduct to pass with impunity."[15] In order to steward the officer corps, Wayne also approved the dismissal of Lieutenants St. Thomas Jenifer and Hastings Marks as well as Captain John Sullivan for issues dealing with drunkenness. Wayne dismissed Lieutenant William Smith for repeatedly being absent from parade and for treating a superior with contempt. Captain Joseph Shaylor suffered dismissal for an unspecified "breach of military propriety." Captain Jacob Melcher resigned in lieu of dismissal for dereliction of duty after abandoning the supply convoy he commanded, and Ensign William Gassaway received a reprimand for "wearing clothing not uniform at the head of his guard."[16] Captain Ballard Smith received a six-month suspension for conduct "unlike a Gentleman and Officer and repugnant to the dignity of the army" by keeping a sergeant's wife in his own tent; failing to learn his lesson, Smith was dismissed from the Legion less than a year later for intoxication while on duty and related offenses.[17]

Accountability became real enough within the officer corps that Lieutenant William Clark bemoaned to his journal the risk of being "ruined forever" by a single mistake, noting shortly after the battle of Fallen Timbers that the officer of the day had discovered his (Clark) forgetting to issue countersigns to his sentries. If this officer, noted Clark, "had me arrested, I should have been Broke, unquestionably. I can but be astonished to View what a little fault will ruin an officer in the Army."[18] Such representative cases indicate both how serious Army senior leaders were about developing an officer corps that could be trusted to lead the nation's Army and what a struggle it was to develop such a body of officers in the 1790's environment.

Officers throughout the Army hierarchy needed to accept and embrace the requirement to self-regulate the profession if the vision of an officer corps comprised of leaders of character and ability was to be implemented. There are strong indications that many officers did exactly that. The frequent intervention by small groups of officers in disputes between fellow officers indicates a concern for the long-term good of the organization.[19] Captain Samuel Newman's representative journal entry while on St. Clair's 1791 campaign demonstrates such internalization. Newman regrets that "a too strong propensity to liquor, has repeatedly prevented my placing the confidence I ever wish to repose" in a soldier unsuccessfully seeking the captain's support in earning an officer's commission.[20] The recurring presence of these types of incidents in primary sources indicates, of course, both a failure to live up to this ideal and a dedication by leaders to root out such violations.

The second major pattern demonstrated by the early officer corps in terms of stewardship was an evident concern in mentoring and developing young officers through the personal involvement of more senior officers. In an era when leader development commenced only with the arrival of a new officer to the unit, such personal leadership and mentorship was essential to stewardship of the officer corps. It is difficult to know how frequently or how well this took place; primary sources tend not to focus on such matters. However, there are indications that some leaders understood the critical need to develop younger officers through personal engagement. Ensign Hugh Brady related one such incident shortly after his arrival as a new officer of the Legion. Describing his first duty, commanding a guard of pickets, Brady wrote, "The officer of the day, Major Mills, saw, at guard mounting, that I was very green, and when he visited my guard, at twelve o'clock, he took much pains to instruct me. . . The major complimented me, and remained with me for some time. His treatment had the effect to inspire me with the confidence which is indispensable in a young officer, to enable him to perform any duty in a suitable manner."[21]

Both Harmar and St. Clair clearly mentored their fellow Pennsylvanian, Lieutenant Ebenezer Denny, taking a long-term interest in the young officer dating from his service in the Revolutionary War as a teenage ensign. In fact, it seems likely that they were involved in selecting Denny for the honor of planting the flag atop a British redoubt after the victory at Yorktown in 1781.[22] Harmar selected Denny as his adjutant for the 1790 offensive; writing to Knox in its aftermath, Harmar demonstrated his care for an officer he highly valued, noting, "It will afford me great satisfaction to know that some mark of honor will be shown to him (Denny)."[23] Upon Harmar's recommendation, Denny became St. Clair's aide-de-camp for the 1791 campaign, during which he continued to provide advice and counsel to the lieutenant. Denny's almost filial respect and devotion to Harmar emerges from his letters, indicating the close and influential relationship between the two officers, further demonstrated by Denny naming two of his sons, Harmar and St. Clair.[24]

Similarly, Harmar identified Captain John Armstrong as an especially able and effective junior officer, taking a special interest in the development of his fellow Revolutionary War veteran. Harmar selected Armstrong for progressively more demanding missions between 1788 and 1790, offering advice and assistance throughout, while ensuring that the young officer received notice at high levels for his contributions to the Army.[25] Though driven from the officer corps by Wilkinson in 1791, Armstrong's continued correspondence with Harmar also indicates a filial devotion and respect for his former commander.[26] Harmar's continued interest and intervention on behalf of Armstrong indicates Harmar's mentorship and sense of stewardship for both an individual and for the officer corps.[27]

General Wayne developed close and mentoring relationships with young officers like Lieutenant William Henry Harrison. Recognizing the junior officer's education, dedication, and bravery, Wayne plucked Harrison from a detachment command to serve as his aide-de-camp in 1793. Following the battle of Fallen Timbers, Wayne singled Harrison out for praise to Knox, before granting the future president the much-desired assignment as Fort Washington commander in 1795. Wayne's "deep fondness" for Harrison manifested itself in assurances of the latter's prospects in the Army – promises which kept him in the Army until after Wayne's 1796 death. [28] Other officers, like Captains Henry DeButts and William Clark became Wayne protégées, developing strong relationships with the commanding general demonstrated by his continued interventions in their careers until his death.[29]

It is probably dangerous to draw from these few examples generalities concerning concepts of mentorship across the officer corps, but they do indicate an understanding by some senior officers of the importance of personal leadership in identifying and guiding promising officers. At the same time, these examples indicate patterns of junior officers looking for mentors to guide and direct their continued progression in the profession.

Stewardship in the early American officer corps drew heavily from the example and input of George Washington. Senior Army leaders during his presidency adopted his concern for the power of officers' examples and in a satisfactory level of military performance and ethical character within the officer corps. Focusing on accountability and discipline, the officer corps attempted with some degree of success to regulate and police members, trying to ensure that only those deserving the title of officer served in that role. Lacking any institutional means of leader development, leaders turned to personal relationships to develop promising officers. Substantial obstacles, many not of the officers corps' making, yet real nonetheless, limited all of these efforts at effectively shaping the officer corps of the future. Thus, stewardship remained a work in progress for the republic's early officer corps.

Notes

1.   Headquarters, Department of the Army, ADP 1, para. 2-24; discussion of stewardship that follows this note comes from paras. 2-24 through 2-27, as well as Headquarters, Department of the Army, *Whitepaper - Our Army Profession,* 13.

2.   Headquarters, Department of the Army, ADP 1, para. 2-26.

3.   See the chapter in this thesis on service for a description of the way officers restricted their view of professionalism to the officer corps.

4.   Ward, *The Department of War,* describes the competing demands for a very limited force.

5.   See description of difficulty of protecting students and negative impact on the West Point school in Wade, 59-61 and in correspondence between Wayne and Secretary of War Timothy Pickering in June 1795, found in Knopf, *Anthony Wayne,* 429, 434.

6.   The best and most comprehensive source for a discussion of the process of Army expansion and contraction throughout Washington's presidency is Kohn, *Eagle and Sword.*

7.   Knopf, *Anthony Wayne*, Wayne to Knox, 15 January 1793, 171.

8.   Data on fort staffing is drawn from various officer reports in official correspondence, from officer journals stationed at particular posts, and from reports quoted in Guthman and Gaff.

9.   Ward, *The Department of War,* convincingly describes the institutional limitations of the department during this period.

10. Correspondence between Wayne and Knox and Pickering clearly show all were aware of Wilkinson's secret and treasonous conniving with Spanish authorities and suspected him of attempting to undermine the effectiveness of the Legion by interfering with logistical operations. The administration's response to ignore such actions is at first glance inexplicable. Yet, as both Linklater and Kohn, "General Wilkinson's Vendetta with General Wayne" convincingly argue, Washington and his officials reasoned that political necessities, including keeping Wilkinson relatively quiet, overrode demands for justice and accountability.

11. John C. Fitzpatrick, ed., *The Writings of George Washington*, vol. III (Washington, DC: Government Printing Office, 1944), 441.

12. Examples of officer dismissal for perceived misconduct drawn from a sample from George Washington, "Washington's General Orders," *George Washington Papers,* Alderman Library, University of Virginia, Charlottesville, VA, 14 March 1778, http://gwpapers.virginia.edu (accessed 7 May 2013) and from Stuart Bernath, "George Washington and the Genesis of American Military Discipline," *Mid-America: An Historical Review* 49, no. 2 (April 1967): 90.

13. Knopf, *Anthony Wayne*, Knox to Wayne, 7 August 1792, 63.

14. Thornbrough, *Outpost on the Wabash,* Harmar to Jeffers, 27 August 1790, 253.

15. Knopf, *Orderly Books for the United States Legion*, July, 1792, 6.

16. Knopf, various entries between 1792 and 1794, 6-88.

17. Gaff, 65, 160-162.

18. Clark, 441. The number of second chances offered to officers is striking and indicates Clark's claim here is overstated, yet his concern in his journal describes an important perception.

19. The previous chapter of this thesis, on esprit, describes such interventions.

20. Newman, 6.

21. Brady's history and reminisces recounted in Linn, 222.

22. Colonel Richard Butler selected Denny but it seems as officers in the same Pennsylvania Line, both Harmar and St. Clair were at least aware, if not involved. See Denny, 10.

23. Denny, intro. 16.

24. Denny, 15-16, 28, 257-273.

25. See series of letters from 1789-1790 between Harmar, Armstrong and Hamtramck indicating this type of relationship in Thornbrough, *Outpost on the Wabash*, 173-177, 196.

26. Correspondence in Armstrong reveals his sense of persecution, stemming from his refusal to join the coterie of officers around Wilkinson. Kohn comes to the same conclusion, that Armstrong was unfairly driven from the officer corps by a vengeful Wilkinson in *Eagle and Sword*, 179.

27. In Armstrong, multiple original letters between Harmar and Armstrong reveal this close relationship.

28. Booraem, 137, 159.

29. Knopf, *Anthony Wayne*, Wayne to Pickering, 19 September 1795, 460; and Jones, 88.

Chapter 8
Conclusion

In the summer of 1792, Captain Henry Carbery issued written guidance to Lieutenant Benjamin Price as the lieutenant marched a detachment of newly recruited Soldiers off to join the Army as it prepared for offensive operations. Carbery wrote:

> I recommend to you the most kind and gentle treatment to your men, and the most unexceptionable conduct towards the inhabitants of the country, through which you may pass – the first, are your brother Soldiers, with whom, in all probability, you will have to encounter savages and perhaps, to bleed again in defense of the helpless – the others, peaceful citizens, who will treat you with civility, if they are not afraid of your company . . . My utmost exertions have been used to accommodate the men, under your command, to military order and discipline – and to impress them, by every means in my power, with a proper sense of their important duty, and a ready and willing obedience to the dictates of their officers.[1]

In this one short missive, Carbery demonstrated a profound understanding of the demands placed upon an officer corps serving the new American republic. His guidance reveals a strong appreciation for the critical importance of a profession of arms based upon civil-military and internal-Army trust, military order and discipline, selfless service, and a sense of both esprit and stewardship.

A similar and generally widespread appreciation developed within the early officer corps between 1789 and 1796, revealing a real anticipation of the Army's current doctrine on military professionalism, with its focus on trust, expertise, service, esprit, and stewardship as the key characteristics of an Army professional. This similarity refutes the notion, implied by some scholars, that the experience of the officer corps of the late eighteenth century has little relevance for understanding the challenges facing the modern American military professional.[2] Therefore the early officer corps, sharing an appreciation for these five key characteristics of professionalism and facing some of the same fundamental challenges confronting officers today, can and should provide historical insight into a deep understanding of military professionalism.

Among the many possible syntheses able to be drawn from this study of the early officer corps, five are particularly relevant today, for they are extracted from the officer corps in the 1790s grappling with realities or tensions still challenging the modern military professional. First, Army leaders emerged from the Revolutionary War and Confederation era convinced of the need for a reliable military establishment able to fully meet security requirements without sacrificing the ideological values of the American republic. The need to ensure ideological reliability committed Washington and Knox, and nearly all other national leaders, to a central role for trained state militia forces in ensuring American national security. The requirement for military expertise, so evident in the Revolution and in frontier conflicts in the decade following the 1783 Treaty of Paris, led leaders like Washington and Knox to simultaneously emphasize the value and need of a regular and permanent body of regulars, led by officers "well skilled in the Theory and Art of War, who will be ready on any occasion, to mix and diffuse their knowledge of Discipline to other Corps . . ."[3]

This mixed force, composed of both federal and state forces, operated together throughout the Northwest Indian War. Its drastic failures early in the war led some to doubt the vision of trained state units integrated with regular forces, providing a reliable and effective Army. Many in the federal Army officer corps possessed such doubts, just as they had during the Revolution, especially in the aftermath of the disastrous 1790 and 1791 offensives against the confederation of hostile northwest area tribes.[4] Yet in the end, these struggles failed to shake the idea of a need for a mixed military establishment comprised of both federal and state military forces. In fact, the victory at Fallen Timbers reinforced the widely-shared perception that a well-led non-regular force could be effective, especially when acting in conjunction with federal elements. Through the course of this campaign, General Wayne's officer corps developed a grudging appreciation for the contribution from the Kentucky mounted volunteers. To many Americans, the skillful synchronization of forces by Wayne and Kentucky's General Charles Scott ultimately validated the vision of Washington and Knox - that an effective militia force joined cohesively with regulars was the military establishment best suited to meet both the security and ideological needs of the American republic. Secretary of War James McHenry articulated this understanding in 1796, arguing to Congress that militia formations, central to the nation's defense, benefited deeply from a regular Army that ought to serve as "a model and school for an army, (with) experienced officers to form it, in case of war."[5] By the conclusion of the war in 1795, a general willingness developed, across the mainstream political spectrum, to accept the legitimacy of this mixed force concept. This critical development obviously provides insight into the modern Army's total force concept, in which active Army, National Guard, and Army reserve forces constitute one Army.

Second, led by President George Washington and Secretary Henry Knox, the Army officer corps fully accepted and internalized the need to find a balance between the potentially conflicting principles of civil-military trust and military expertise. Only socially and politically trustworthy officers could be depended upon to use the military expertise and power gathered in the federal officer corps. Only such officers could be trusted to act in defense of, and never in undermining, American values of individual liberty and justice. Officers proved their trustworthiness not by their rank or position, but by their demonstration of selfless service, commitment to the greater cause of the republic, their military ability, and care for those whose lives were entrusted to them. Only after officers demonstrated the competence, commitment and character worthy of the role of leading free American citizens, could they demand the discipline, order, and deference required of an effective Army. This key realization among early Army leaders and officers led directly to the push to implement high standards of leader accountability and a focus on the importance of strong character among Army officers. Thus, officers during Washington's presidency sought to seamlessly integrate and synchronize trust and expertise, realizing that the existence of one of these characteristics without the other failed to meet both the security and ideological needs of the American republic. The need to balance trust and expertise, as *The Army* emphasizes, remains today.

Third, Army officers considered their military officership as an extension of their role as societal leaders. Largely rejecting the more modern notion of the professional benefits of at least some separation from the larger society, early American Army officers engaged with society both in width and depth.[6] As described earlier in this thesis, military officers participated deeply in their society while often practicing a wide variety of leadership roles outside the officer corps. William Henry Harrison is a superb example of this. While stationed at Fort Washington just outside the town of Cincinnati, Lieutenant Harrison remained deeply engaged in civilian society, supporting the building of a town church, partnering with local civilians to form a distillery business, and courting and marrying a local woman.[7] After his service as a junior officer between 1792 and 1798, Harrison gained fame holding leadership position as territorial secretary and governor, War of 1812 general, congressman, ambassador, and finally president. While the level of Harrison's leadership roles was obviously unusual, officers of the Army of the 1790s commonly held leadership positions outside of their Army service. This connection to civilian society was crucial to the sense of trust deemed so necessary by

Army leaders during this era. Officers that were engaged as American citizens and active in civilian affairs proved the legitimacy of their claim to be faithful citizen-Soldiers. Such officer engagement in the larger society resulted in a network of citizen-Soldiers interwoven into American society, simultaneously focused on protecting the country and establishing a foundation of trust between the military and American society. In the current age, many worry about a widening gap between the military and American society while others express concern about the involvement of officers in political affairs. In light of the continued requirement to think through the American military officer's place in the larger society, the early officer corps' approach to issues related to trust and service may provide important insights.[8]

Fourth, a sense of instability and a lack of resources in the early officer corps limited consistent career-service, a winning spirit, and the development of institutional vehicles by which principles of expertise, esprit, and stewardship could be especially nourished. The political and economic environment of the 1790s had a profound influence on the development of the early Army officer corps, limiting stability and the manpower, talent, time, and financial resources available to the officer corps between 1789 and 1796. Army leaders responded to this reality by consistently prioritizing the immediate mission requirements of defeating hostile Indian tribes over a longer-term focus on promoting military expertise, stable patterns of service, and shaping the officer corps of the future through stewardship. As discussed in the previous chapter, attempts by the Washington administration and the Army to found an institution devoted to the education of future artillery and engineer officers withered in the face of an unstable and constraining environment. The near-constant threat of reductions in the officer corps and slight reductions in the number and rank of officers in the aftermath of the Fallen Timbers victory decreased esprit and motivation for both career-service and serious dedication to stewardship among Army leaders. A lack of stability within the Army over the last decade is now joined by an environment characterized by constrained resources, potentially impacting levels of expertise, esprit, and stewardship among Army officers. Facing similar types of issues in the 1790s, the response of Army officers may provide historically relevant insights.

Finally, it is important to recognize that the influence of George Washington on the officer corps in the 1790s was profound and far-reaching. In many ways, the story of the officer corps during his presidency is a tale of the organization seeking to implement Washington's vision for officers. Through his Revolutionary War leadership, so intimately familiar to almost all of the field grade officers serving the country in the 1790s, his example and his guidance, the president focused the attention of civilian and military leaders on his vision for American officership. Washington erected this vision on a foundation of respect for the need to form a particularly American Army officer corps, acceptable to the ideals of a free people, while still being able to provide military expertise in leading an effective defense establishment. His ideal and example of selfless service reverberated throughout the military establishment, decisively impacting the ethos of the officer corps of the 1790s. Washington's Revolutionary War leadership of officers centered on forming a band of brothers-in-arms, with powerful ties of loyalty and a commitment to the cause. His devotion to civil control of the military decisively implemented an enduring and foundational American military and political principle. Finally, his emphasis on officer character and accountability provided an enduring example for officers in the 1790s.[9] Because of Washington's powerful influence, it is no real surprise that the five elements chosen by current Army leaders to characterize today's military professional were critical elements of Washington's example and vision for American officership. While the study of such figures as Carl Von Clausewitz and Antoine-Henri Jomini remains important, it may be useful to consider equally Washington's understanding of warfare and his deep influence on American military thought. Without peer in inspiring the development of the American military tradition, Washington, and his understanding of trust, expertise, service, esprit, and stewardship, seems highly worthy of the attention of officers seeking to better comprehend American military professionalism.

Scholars have expended much effort in disputes regarding when military professionalism developed in the United States military. Some have disputed whether or not officers of the late eighteenth century deserve the appellation of military professional.[10] In the end, it matters little how the Army officer corps of the 1790s is defined, whether they are depicted as military professionals, semi-professionals, or amateurs. A focus on the professional status of these officers is likely to revolve around semantic distinctions and misses the larger point. What is historically important and relevant is the recognition that in its most formative years, between 1789 and 1796, the officer corps of the United States confronted issues relating to trust, military expertise, honorable service, esprit, and stewardship. In doing so, officers often developed patterns and practices that were legitimate expressions of a profession of arms, expressing and revealing growing competence, dedicated commitment, and a striving to live up to the demands of character. These expressions, while developed over 200 years ago, still provide a useful background for military professionals today.

A study of the early officer corps is especially relevant to American military officers, for these officers developed a sense of professionalism that was, in some ways, uniquely American. Developed in the early national period, and deeply influenced by the Revolutionary War heritage, the officer corps' expressions of professionalism confronted and ultimately accepted the ideological, political, and social concerns of the young American republic. Sharing with today's officer corps a requirement to grapple with the inherent tensions and necessary balances relating to trust, expertise, service, esprit, and stewardship, the experience of officers like Captain Henry Carbery, like those serving at Kekionga in 1790, along the Wabash in 1791 and at Fallen Timbers in 1794, provide a useful framework to better grasp the core meaning of American military professionalism.

Notes

1. Gaff, Carbery to Price, 3 July 1792, 38.

2. For instance, Huntington judges that before the mid-nineteenth century, the amateurism of the officer corps negates any real relevance to the modern military professional.

3. Washington, "Sentiments on a Peace Establishment."

4. See the chapter in this thesis on military expertise for a discussion of the regular officer corps' perception of state militia and volunteers units.

5. United States, *American State Papers, Military Affairs,* McHenry Report to Congressional Committee, 14 March 1796, 112.

6. For a strong depiction of this modern idea, see the argument that the relative isolation of the American officer corps in the decades following the Civil War was highly beneficial to the development of military professionalism in Huntington.

7. Booraem, 90, 159-161, 164.

8. Many influential scholars and observers have relatively recently commented on a growing civil-military gap. Included among such are Richard Kohn and Peter Feaver, *Soldiers and Civilians: The Civil-Military Gap and American National Security,* (Cambridge, MA: MIT Press, 2001) and Tom Ricks, "The Widening Gap between Military and Society," *The Atlantic,* 1 July, 1997, http://www.theatlantic.com/magazine/archive/1997/07/the-widening-gap-between-military-and-society/306158/ (8 May 2013). The current Chairman of the JCS, General Martin Dempsey, has consistently expressed concerns about the need for the officer corps to remain apolitical.

9. Washington's vision and influence on the later officer corps is described throughout this thesis. I have drawn my understanding of Washington from his papers and multiple secondary sources. Most influential of the latter, and I think the best single discussion of Washington's sense of leadership and professionalism, is Higginbotham, *George Washington and the American Military Tradition.*

10. See the historiography in this thesis for a description of these discussions.

Bibliography

Primary Sources

Armstrong, John. *The John Armstrong Papers.* Indianapolis, IN: Indiana Historical Society, n.d.

Boyer, Lieutenant. *A Journal of Wayne's Campaign. Being an Authentic Daily Record of the Most Important Occurrences During the Campaign of Major General Anthony Wayne, against the Northwestern Indians.* Cincinnati, OH: Printed for W. Dodge, by J. F. Uhlhorn, 1866.

Bradley, Daniel and Frazer E. Wilson. *Journal of Capt. Daniel Bradley; An Epic of the Ohio Frontier.* Greenville, OH: F. H. Jobes & Son, 1935.

Buell, John Hutchinson. *The Diary of John Hutchison Buell.* Edited by Richard Knopf. Columbus, OH: Anthony Wayne Parkway Board, Ohio State Museum, 1957.

Butterfield, Consul W., ed. *Journal of Capt. Jonathan Heart on the March with His Company from Connecticut to Fort Pitt, in Pittsburgh, Pennsylvania, from the Seventh of September, to the Twelfth of October, 1785.* Albany, NY: J. Munsell's Sons, 1885.

Clark, William. "William Clark's Journal of General Wayne's Campaign." Edited by R. C. McGrane. *Mississippi Valley Historical Review* 1 (December 1914): 418-444.

Denny, Ebenezer. *Military Journal of Major Ebenezer Denny.* Philadelphia, PA: J. B. Lippincott & Co., 1860.

Harmar, Josiah. *The Proceedings of a Court of Inquiry, held at the special request of Brigadier General Josiah Harmar, Commanding Officer of the Expedition against the Miami Indians, 1790.* Philadelphia, PA: John Fenno, 1791.

Heckewelder, John G. *History, Manners, and Customs of the Indian Nations Who Once Inhabited Pennsylvania and Neighboring States.* New York, NY: Arno Press, 1971.

Johonnet, Jackson. *The Remarkable Adventures of Jackson Johonnet of Massachusetts, Who Served as a Soldier in the Western Army, in the Massachusetts Line, in the Expedition under General Harmar, and the Unfortunate General St. Clair, Containing an Account of His Captivity, Sufferings, and Escape from the Kickapoo Indians.* Boston, MA: S. Hall, 1793.

Knopf, Richard C., ed. *Anthony Wayne, a Name in Arms: Soldier, Diplomat, Defender of Expansion Westward of a Nation; the Wayne-Knox-Pickering-McHenry Correspondence*. Westport, CT: Greenwood Press, 1975.

_____. *Orderly Books for the United States Legion Vols. I-IV Incl.* Columbus, OH: Anthony Wayne Parkway Board, Ohio State Museum, 1955.

_____. *A Surgeon's Mate at Fort Defiance: The Journal of Joseph Gardner Andrews for the Year 1795*. Columbus, OH: Ohio Historical Society, 1957.

Linn, John B., ed. "Reminiscences of Hugh Brady." In *Annals of Buffalo Valley, Pennsylvania, 1755-1855*. 219-231. Harrisburg, PA: L. S. Hart, printer, 1877.

Miller, Edward. *With Captain Edward Miller in the Wayne Campaign of 1794*. Edited by Dwight L. Smith. Ann Arbor, MI: William L. Clements Library, 1965.

Newman, Samuel. "A Picture of the First United States Army: The Journal of Captain Samuel Newman." Edited by Milo M. Quaife. *Wisconsin Magazine of History* 2 (September 1918): 40-73.

Quaife, Milo M., ed. "Fort Knox Orderly Book, 1793-97." *Indiana Magazine of History* 32, no. 2 (1936): 137-169.

Sargent, Winthrop. *Diary of Colonel Winthrop Sargent, Adjutant General of the United States Army, During the Campaign of 1791*. Wormsloe, GA: publisher, 1851.

Smith, Dwight L., ed. *From Greene Ville to Fallen Timbers: A Journal of the Wayne Campaign*. Indianapolis, IN: Indiana Historical Society, 1952.

Smith, William H., ed. *The St. Clair Papers: The Life and Public Services of Arthur St. Clair : Soldier of the Revolutionary War, President of the Continental Congress ; and Governor of the North-Western Territory with His Correspondence and Other Papers*. 2 vols. Cincinnati, OH: R. Clarke, 1882.

St. Clair, Arthur. *A Narrative of the Manner in Which the Campaign Against the Indians, in the Year One Thousand, Seven Hundred and Ninety one, Was Conducted, Under the Command of Major-General St. Clair*. Philadelphia, PA: Jane Aitken, 1812.

Steuben, Friedrich Wilhelm Ludolf Gerhard Augustin. *Baron Von Steuben's Revolutionary War Drill Manual.* 1794. Reprint, New York, NY: Dover Publications, 1985.

Thornbrough, Gayle, ed. *Outpost on the Wabash, 1787-1791; Letters of Brigadier General Josiah Harmar and Major John Francis Hamtramck. and Other Letters and Documents* Indianapolis, IN: Indiana Historical Society, 1957.

Underwood, Thomas T. *Journal, Thomas Taylor Underwood, March 26, 1792 to March 18, 1800: An Old Soldier in Wayne's Army.* Cincinnati, OH: Society of Colonial Wars in the State of Ohio, 1945.

United States. *American State Papers, Indian Affairs, Volume I.* New York, NY: Arno, 1979.

_____. *American State Papers, Military Affairs, Volume I.* New York, NY: Arno, 1979.

Washington, George. *The George Washington Papers.* Alderman Library, University of Virginia, Charlottesville, VA. http://rotunda.upress. virginia.edu/founders/GEWN (accessed 7 May 2013).

Wayne, Anthony. "Roster of the Officers of the Legion of the United States Commanded by Major-General Anthony Wayne." The *Pennsylvania Magazine of History and Biography* 16, no. 4 (January, 1893): 423-429.

Wayne, Anthony and Richard C. Knopf. *A Precise Journal of General Wayne's Last Campaign.* Worcester, MA: American Antiquarian Society, 1954.

Wilkinson, James. "General James Wilkinson's Narrative of the Fallen Timbers Campaign." Edited by Milo Quaife. *Mississippi Valley Historical Review* 16 (June 1929): 81-90.

Secondary Sources

Ambrose, Stephen E. *Upton and the Army.* Baton Rouge, LA: Louisiana State University Press, 1964.

Backus, Emma. "Cornelius Sedam and his Friends in Washington's Time." *Ohio Archaeological and Historical Quarterly* 41, no. 1 (January 1932): 37-48.

Bald, F. Clever. "Colonel John Francis Hamtramck." *Indiana Magazine of History* 44 (December 1948): 335-354.

Beatty, Joseph M. ed. "Letters of the Four Beatty Brothers." *Pennsylvania Magazine of History and Biography* 44, no. 3 (1920): 192-263.

Bernath, Stuart. "George Washington and the Genesis of American Military Discipline." *Mid-America: An Historical Review* 49, no. 2 (April 1967): 90.

Bonney, Catharina Vissher. *A Legacy of Historical Gleanings*. Albany, NY: J. Munsell, 1875.

Booraem, Hendrik. *A Child of the Revolution: William Henry Harrison and His World, 1773-1798*. Kent, OH: Kent State University Press, 2012.

Brown, Allan S. "The Role of the Army in Western Settlement: Josiah Harmar's Command, 1785-1790." *Pennsylvania Magazine of History and Biography* 93 (April 1969): 161-178.

Butler, William David, John Cromwell Butler, and Joseph Marion Butler. *The Butler Family in America*. St. Louis, MO: Shallcross Print. Co., 1909.

Carp, E. Wayne. "The Problem of National Defense in the Early American Republic." In *The American Revolution: Its Character and Limits*. Edited by Jack Green. 14-50. New York, NY: New York University Press, 1987.

Coffman, Edward M. "The Duality of the American Military Tradition: A Commentary." *Journal of Military History* 64 (2000): 967-980.

_____. *The Old Army: A Portrait of the American Army in Peacetime, 1784-1898*. Oxford, UK: Oxford University Press, 1986.

Cress, Lawrence D. *Citizens in Arms: The Army and the Militia in American Society to the War of 1812*. Chapel Hill, NC: University of North Carolina Press, 1982.

Cunliffe, Marcus. *Soldiers and Civilians: The Martial Spirit in America, 1775-1865*. Boston, MA: Little and Brown, 1968.

Currie, James T. "The First Congressional Investigation: St. Clair's Military Disaster of 1791." *Parameters* 20 (December 1990): 95-102.

Depuy Trevor and R. Ernest Depuy. *Military Heritage of America*. New York, NY: McGraw-Hill, 1956.

Downes, Randolph C. *Frontier Ohio, 1788-1803*. Columbus, OH: Ohio State Archaeological and Historical Society, 1935.

Eid, Leroy V. "American Indian Military Leadership: St. Clair's 1791 Defeat." *Journal of Military History* 57 (January 1993): 71-88.

Fischer, Joseph R. *A Well-Executed Failure: The Sullivan Campaign against the Iroquois, July-September 1779.* Columbia, SC: University of South Carolina Press, 1997.

Fitzpatrick David. "Emory Upton and the Citizen Soldier." *The Journal of Military History* 65 (April 2001): 355-389.

Fitzpatrick, John C., ed., *The Writings of George Washington,* vol. III. Washington, DC: Government Printing Office, 1944.

Fredriksen, John C. "A Tempered Sword Untested: the Military Career of General George Izard (Part I)." *The Journal of America's Military Past* 25, no. 2 (Fall, 1998): 7.

_____. *The United States Army in the War of 1812: Concise Biographies of Commanders and Operational Histories of Regiments, with Bibliographies of Published and Primary Resources.* Jefferson, NC: McFarland & Co., 2009.

Gaff, Alan D. *Bayonets in the Wilderness: Anthony Wayne's Legion in the Old Northwest.* Norman, OK: University of Oklahoma Press, 2004.

Gairdner, Asa Bird. "Henry Burbeck: Brevet Brigadier-General United States Army--Founder of the United States Military Academy." *Magazine of American History* 9 (April 1883): 251-265.

Ganoe, William. *History of the United States Army.* New York, NY: D. Appleton-Century Co., 1942.

Greene, Jack P. *The American Revolution: Its Character and Limits.* New York, NY: New York University Press, 1987.

Gunderson, Robert G. "William Henry Harrison: Apprentice in Arms." *Northwest Ohio Quarterly* 65 (Winter 1993): 3-29.

Guthman, William H. *March to Massacre; A History of the First Seven Years of the United States Army, 1784-1791.* New York, NY: McGraw Hill, 1975.

Headquarters, Department of the Army. Army Doctrine Publication 1, *The Army.* Washington, DC: Government Printing Office, September, 2012. http://armypubs.army.mil/doctrine/ADP_1.html (accessed 12 May 2013).

_____. *Whitepaper - Our Army Profession* (Draft). Washington, DC: Government Printing Office, 24 March 2012.

Headquarters, Army Training and Doctrine Command. *The Army Profession: 2012, After More than a Decade of Conflict.* Center for the Army Profession and Ethic, October 2011. http://cape.army.mil/repository/ProArms/Army%20Profession%20Pamphlet.pdf (accessed 12 May 2013).

_____. *America's Army – Our Profession Information Paper,* Center for the Army Profession and Ethic, October 2012. http://cape.army.mil/AAOP/AAOP%20Overview/repository/info%20paper/20121004_AA-OP_Information_Paper_(Final_Approved_v2).pdf (accessed 12 May 2013).

Heitman, Francis B. *Historical Register and Dictionary of the United States Army: from its Organization, September 29, 1789, to March 2, 1903.* Washington, DC: Government Printing Office, 1903.

Higginbotham, Don."American Historians and the Military History of the American Revolution." *The American Historical Review* 70 (October, 1964): 18-34.

_____. "The Early American Way of War: Reconnaissance and Appraisal." *The William and Mary Quarterly* 44, no. 2 (April 1987): 230-273.

_____. *George Washington and the American Military Tradition.* Athens, GA: University of Georgia Press, 1985.

_____. *George Washington Reconsidered.* Charlottesville, VA: University of Virginia Press, 2001.

Huntington, Samuel P. *The Soldier and the State: The Theory and Politics of Civil-Military Relations.* Cambridge, MA: Belknap Press of Harvard University, 1957.

Hurt, R. Douglas. *The Ohio Frontier: Crucible of the Old Northwest, 1720-1830.* Bloomington, IN: Indiana University Press, 1996.

Jacobs, James Ripley. *The Beginning of the US Army, 1783-1812.* Princeton, NJ: Princeton University Press, 1947.

Jones, Landon Y. *William Clark and the Shaping of the West.* New York, NY: Hill and Wang, 2004.

Katzenberger, George A. "Major David Zeigler." *Ohio Archaeological and Historical Quarterly* 21 (April-July 1912): 127-174.

Kohn, Richard H. *Eagle and Sword: The Federalists and the Creation of the Military Establishment in America, 1783-1802.* New York, NY: Free Press, 1975.

_____. "General Wilkinson's Vendetta with General Wayne: Politics and Command in the American Army, 1791-1796." *Filson Club Historical Quarterly* 45 (October 1971): 361-372.

Kohn, Richard and Peter Feaver. *Soldiers and Civilians: The Civil-Military Gap and American National Security.* Cambridge, MA: MIT Press, 2001.

Kretchik, Walter E. *US Army Doctrine: From the American Revolution to the War on Terror.* Lawrence, KS: University Press of Kansas, 2011.

Lee, Wayne E. "Early American Ways of War: A New Reconnaissance, 1600-1815." *The Historical Journal* 44, I (2001): 269-289.

Linklater, Andro. *An Artist in Treason: The Extraordinary Double Life of General James Wilkinson.* New York, NY: Walker, 2009.

Lockhart, Paul D. *The Drillmaster of Valley Forge: The Baron De Steuben and the Making of the American Army.* Washington, DC: Smithsonian, 2008.

Mahon, John. "Pennsylvania and the Beginnings of the Regular Army." *Pennsylvania History* 21 (January 1954): 42.

Metcalf, Bryce. *Original Members and Other Officers Eligible to the Society of the Cincinnati, 1783-1938, With the Institution, Rules of Admission and Lists of the Officers of the General and State Societies.* Strasburg, VA: Shenandoah Pub., 1938.

Millett, Allan R. "Caesar and the Northwest: The Wayne Campaign 1792-1795." *Timeline* 14, no. 3 (May 1997): 2-21.

_____. *Military Professionalism and Officership in America.* Columbus, OH: Mershon Center of the Ohio State University, 1977.

Murray, J. A. "The Butlers of Cumberland Valley," *Historical Register: Notes and Queries* I (January 1883).

_____. "The Butler Family of the Pennsylvania Line." *The Pennsylvania Magazine of History and Biography* 7, no. 1 (1883): 1-6.

Myers, Minor. *Liberty without Anarchy: A History of the Society of the Cincinnati* Charlottesville, VA: University of Virginia Press, 1983.

Nelson, Paul D. *Anthony Wayne: Soldier of the Early Republic.* Bloomington, IN: Indiana University Press, 1985.

_____. "General Charles Scott, the Kentucky Mounted Volunteers, and the Northwest Indian Wars, 1784-1794." *Journal of the Early Republic* 6, no. 3 (Fall 1986): 219-251.

Odon, William O. "Destined for Defeat: An Analysis of the St. Clair Expedition of 1791." *Northwest Ohio Quarterly* 65 (Spring 1993): 68-93.

Palmer, John McAuley. *America in Arms: The Experience of the United States with Military Organization.* New Haven, CT: Yale University Press, 1941.

_____. *Statesmanship or War.* Garden City, NY: Doubleday, 1927.

Peckham, Howard. "Josiah Harmar and His Indian Expedition." *Ohio Archaeological and Historical Quarterly* 55 (July 1946): 227-241.

Powers, Sandra. "Studying the Art of War: Military Books Known to American Officers and Their French Counterparts during the Second Half of the Eighteenth Century." *The Journal of Military History* 70 (July, 2006): 781-814.

"Proceedings of the General Society of the Cincinnati, 1783-1902." Society of Cincinnati's Headquarters, Washington DC

Puls, Mark. *Henry Knox: Visionary General of the American Revolution.* New York, NY: Palgrave Macmillan, 2008.

Ricks, Tom. "The Widening Gap between Military and Society." *The Atlantic,* 1 July 1997, http://www.theatlantic.com/magazine/archive/1997/07/the-widening-gap-between-military-and-society/306158/ (accessed 8 May 2013).

Roosevelt, Theodore. *The Winning of the West, vol. III.* New York, NY: Putnam, 1889.

Rowe, Mary Ellen. *Bulwark of the Republic: The American Militia in Antebellum West.* Westport, CT: Praeger, 2003.

Royster, Charles. *A Revolutionary People at War.* Chapel Hill, NC: University of North Carolina Press, 1979.

Simmons, David A. "The Military and Administrative Abilities of James Wilkinson in the Old Northwest, 1792-1793." *Old Northwest* 3 (September 1977): 237-250.

Skelton, William B. *An American Profession of Arms: The Army Officer Corps, 1784-1861.* Lawrence, KS: University Press of Kansas, 1992.

_____. "Samuel P. Huntington and the Roots of the American Military Tradition." *The Journal of Military History* 60 (April 1996): 325-338.

Steinle, John. "Unlucky Soldier: Josiah Harmar's Frontier Struggle." *Timeline* 8 (April/May 1991): 2-17.

Steward, David. *American Emperor.* New York, NY: Simon and Schuster, 2011.

Storm, Colton. "Lieutenant Armstrong's Expedition to the Missouri River, 1790." *Mid-America An Historical Review* 15 (July 1943): 180-188.

Sword, Wiley. *President Washington's Indian War: The Struggle for the Old Northwest, 1790-1795.* Norman, OK: University of Oklahoma Press, 1985.

Upton, Emory. *The Military Policy of the United States.* Washington, DC: United States Government Printing Office, 1912.

Wade, Arthur P. "Artillerists and Engineers: The Beginnings of American Seacoast Fortifications, 1794-1815." Ph.D. dissertation, Kansas State University, Manhattan, KS, 1977.

Ward, Harry M. *The Department of War, 1781-1795.* Pittsburgh, PA: University of Pittsburgh Press, 1962.

_____. *Charles Scott and the Spirit of '76.* Charlottesville, VA: University of Virginia Press, 1988.

Warner, Michael S. "General Josiah Harmar's Campaign Reconsidered: How the Americans Lost the Battle of Kekionga." *Indiana Magazine of History* 83, no. 1 (March 1987): 41-64.

Weigley, Russell F. *Towards an American Army: Military Thought from Washington to Marshall.* New York, NY: Columbia University Press, 1962.

_____. *History of the United States Army.* New York, NY: MacMillan, 1967.

Weiss, Harry B., and Grace M. Ziegler. *Colonel Erkuries Beatty, 1759-1823.* Trenton, NJ: Past Times Press, 1958.

Wilson, Frazer E. *Arthur St. Clair, Rugged Ruler of the Old Northwest.* Richmond, VA: Garrett and Massie, 1944.

Wood, Gordon S. "The Greatness of George Washington." In *George Washington Reconsidered.* Edited by Don Higginbotham. 309-324. Charlottesville, VA: University of Virginia Press, 2001.

* 9 7 8 1 7 8 2 6 6 5 3 3 5 *